On the Wrong Side of the River

Stories From a Maine Guide

by

Carroll Ware

On the Wrong Side of the River

Copyright © 2022 by Carroll Ware

ISBN 978-1-943424-71-9

LCCN 2022934419

North Country Press
Unity, Maine

—To George Smith, who was instrumental in getting me started with this book, after fifty years of procrastination;

—To The Kid, who convinced me that it was time to put these stories to paper;

—To David, who always wanted me to write;

—To my mother, who must have cringed every time I struck out for the woods, wondering if I'd make it back;

—To Uncle Ken, who taught me how to lay that fly line on the water;

—To the many who over the last sixty or so years have provided some of the moments described in these pages. You have left me with precious and unforgettable moments in time;

—To my beautiful wife, lover, hunting and fishing chum, business partner, frequent supervisor, and the singular most important person in my life, Lila (AKA as the world's most patient woman).

Foreword

I come from several generations of intelligent, articulate people who included Maine guides, woodsmen, loggers, hunters and fishermen, and of all things, schoolteachers. Most of these people all had their roots in the ill-fated village of Flagstaff, Maine. I was blessed to have a single-parent mother who raised me, with considerable help from an aunt and uncle. My mother once told a friend, when speaking about me, that "[she] could take that boy out of the woods, but [she] was NOT going to get the woods out of that boy." Despite her motherly misgivings and constant worry, she had the resolve to turn that little boy loose in the woods. My trips to the wrong side of the river allowed me to discover that often my misadventures gave me the unusual ability to become a pain in my own ass!

One of the constants of my upbringing was humor. Laughter and the understanding that being willing to laugh at oneself would be of great advantage as I grew older, and a lesson that fortunately I acquired early in life.

In all of the years on the way to this point in my life, I have enjoyed a lifetime of experiences and people who were incredibly important to me for many reasons. As I write this, I recently enjoyed my seventy-fifth birthday, and I continue to be amazed at the full and exciting life I have led, one that has provided an endless stream of priceless moment. I have, in my career as a Master Maine Guide and International Travel Consultant with Lila at my side, met so many interesting and sometimes unusual people. Many of those people who were so special to me I have attempted to recognize and honor with this book.

I chose my title for this book simply because I sometimes find myself, literally and otherwise, on the wrong side of the river. It seems that sometimes the water I want to reach is just out of casting distance. Life sometimes parallels fishing in that fishing like life is not always successful the first time. The secret to both is that you have to keep casting.

Table of Contents

My ancestors landed in Orland, Maine, in 1776. Coming from several generations of woodsmen, hunters, fishermen and schoolteachers, I suppose I come by my love of trout fishing naturally. I caught my very first brook trout when I was ten. Little did I know that I would never draw another peaceful breath!

My mother's family all came from the village of Flagstaff in Dead River country. Anyone over the age of fifty is aware of the demise of Flagstaff due to the damming of the Dead River for hydro power. As a kid growing up in Skowhegan, my family made frequent visits to the Stratton and Eustis areas, particularly to Eustis Ridge where many family members owned camps.

The year that I was ten, my ma and grandfather, aunt and uncle and I were going to go to Eustis Ridge above Stratton for a family get-together. We stopped for a picnic above Kingfield at an area named Jerusalem Plantation. The Carrabassett River runs right beside Route 16 for much of the trip and in the plantation in those days there was a state maintained picnic area. The Carrabassett River is one of Maine's most beautiful rivers, with absolutely crystal-clear water. It is one of those places I would fish, even if there weren't any trout there.

Because it was a beautiful sunny summer day, and mostly because we were on the banks of the Carrabassett River, I wanted to fish. To this point in my life, I had never caught a fish of any species with a fly rod. Uncle Bill strung a fly rod for me and added a Parmachenee Belle wet fly to the end of the leader.

Down over the bank I went and made what was my very first cast ("cast" might be a little generous) with a fly rod. Lo and behold a trout rose and swiped at the fly, but missed it. Uncle Bill taught me that if a trout rose and missed, just give it to him again. I cast back to the eddy behind the rock and this time the trout grabbed the fly.

I'd love to say that I carefully and skillfully played the trout to the net, but the truth of the matter is that when he struck, I stiff-heeled him over my shoulder into the bushes behind me. I grabbed the trout and ran up the bank, yelling at the top of my lungs, "Uncle Bill, I think I caught a trout!" The trout was ten inches long and might have been the most important trout that I would ever catch. Little did I know, in my wildest imagination, that when that trout came back the second time and took the fly, in that moment we were both hooked. That trout has remained a great gift and provided one of the most memorable and significant moments in my life.

People who are even older than I am tell me that as you age your short-term memory fades, but you can easily recall events that happened decades ago. This is proving to be the case for me, for I can still see in my mind's eye that trout coming up on my very first cast. I can still recall the vivid color along the side of that first brook trout and the sunlight glimmering as the water ran off that fish.

I have been incredibly fortunate, thanks to our business, Fins and Furs Adventures (notice the shameless plug), to have traveled to some extremely remote, very spectacular places on two continents to fish and hunt. I have caught literally thousands of brook trout, many of them legitimate trophies by any standards up to and including my bucket-list brookie that weighed ten pounds four ounces. That fish was released live and was still swimming the last time I saw him. However, there has not been, and will not be, a more significant trout than the one that the ten-year old boy caught on that beautiful summer day so many years ago.

Looking at my career as a fly fisherman, the old saying that beauty is in the eye of the beholder is true. I have guided dads who were lifelong fly fishermen. I've watched them return with their sons and teach their sons as they were taught. A dad whom I'd guided the previous year returned with number one son for his first trout fishing experience, and dad was moved to tears when his son caught that first trout or salmon on a fly. Odd how the dad happened to have something in his eye and needed to look away just as we netted Junior's first native fish.

To date, I have invested (read "blown") thousands of dollars, hours and efforts in my pursuit of the perfect trout place. I have tied thousands of flies, walked uncountable numbers of miles, fished until I couldn't keep my eyes open, and did it all again the next day.

Fishing continues to bring many, many magical moments to my life, and it all started with that ten-inch trout on the Carrabassett River.

There is something about being on the water or in the Maine woods that has always seemed to calm me. On the morning that my mother died, I left my family at home and went to the woods in the area where I was deer hunting in those days. And, when one of my dearest male friends died, we took his ashes and allowed the waters of the Kennebec River to take him. There is no other place in the world that affects me as Maine does.

At various places in this writing I have mentioned my uncle, a gentleman named Ken Taylor. Uncle Ken was another native son of Flagstaff and was married to my Aunt Olena, and they were both teachers in Flagstaff. Uncle Ken was always more like a father to me than an uncle, and taught me about so many things above and beyond fishing and hunting. I recall occasionally asking questions about topics that were a little too 'mature' for my age or perhaps on a topic that made Uncle Ken a little uncomfortable. He would light his pipe (he always had Middleton Five tobacco) and ponder his answer carefully before sharing his wisdom. He and that pipe were inseparable, evidenced by many little burn holes the tobacco made in sweaters and jackets.

As Ken became older, he was not able to get around as well as he once did. We would sit together and he would share many stories of his years as a young man growing up in Flagstaff. I loved hearing those stories and from them I gained an appreciation for his wisdom and experience. In his days as a hunter and fisherman in the Dead River area, his stories of the numbers of deer and trout left me drooling. He described the number of deer around in those days by sharing that during deer season he, his dad and brothers went into the woods in the morning knowing they would be seeing deer. In his words, "We could pretty much pick the deer that we wanted to shoot."

An old photograph hanging in my den shows Uncle Ken and Gramp standing on a camp porch with a deer hanging that must have weighed in the area of three hundred pounds. The story was told that the deer was so heavy they had to bring up a horse and harness to take that deer off a mountain.

One of the most amazing stories that he told was *how* he and his brothers occasionally hunted deer. When November came the snow deepened as it always did in those days. Sooner or later the deer would finally begin to belly out in the deep snow. My uncles would go into the woods on snowshoes, find a deer track and begin to travel at a fast pace, almost a run. Eventually the deer would begin to tire, the hunter would close the gap with the animal, and they would successfully harvest the deer. As Ken was the first to admit, this was not about the sport of the hunt. This was about feeding families in the dead of winter when food was sometimes in short supply.

The Dead River flowed right through Flagstaff and the trout fishing was tremendous. There were also a dozen or so lakes and ponds in the area that also provided excellent fishing. Spring Lake itself held both brookies and landlocked salmon. In nineteen twenty, Uncle Ken caught a landlocked salmon there that weighed over eight pounds. One of my Uncle's favorite places to fish was the Dead River. There was a large calm area known as a "dead water" somewhere in the Dead River where Ken would describe standing in the moving water with so many trout that as a school of trout swam by, they could be felt brushing against his pants leg.

My mother's maiden name was Viles and in the summers there occasionally would be a big family gathering. This gathering was preceded by the men, including Uncle Ken, making a trout fishing trip to the north branch of the Dead River. Ma related to me many times what wonderful affairs these gatherings were. The men would return from the fishing trip with a couple of pack baskets filled with brook trout. Trout fried in salt pork with hot biscuits, baked in a reflector oven, served with hot tea that would melt the "end of your spoon" was the menu and no one went away hungry.

It amazes me that fish were taken in such large numbers in those days, but as Uncle Ken described it, "This was the way that things were then. We thought that the trout would always be there." In one of my last conversations with Uncle Ken before he passed he told me that in his mind, and the minds of many others of his generation, they had lived through the very best fishing and hunting that Maine has ever seen or will ever see.

Theirs was a remarkable period in Maine's history of hunting, fishing and natural resources. I am so blessed to have had those opportunities to spend time with Ken and relive those memories with him. He was the best man with a fly rod over brook trout that I have ever seen.

Through all of my life I have been very blessed to have enjoyed the friendship of two men who were always very dear to me. They were the brothers that I was never fortunate enough to have and to grow up with. In both cases, we met as school mates and fostered our friendship over the years. I couldn't have chosen two men who were more diverse or different in their approach to life in general and in their personalities.

The Kid, as we have always referred to each other, and I met the spring we were in the seventh grade. We discovered a mutual attraction for fishing and hunting immediately. Our mothers were both schoolteachers and doubtless were blessed with gray hair as a result of our antics at an early age. The year that we were freshmen in high school, the June graduation ceremonies were in full swing and Kid and I decided that, since our school year was at an end, we had no further interest in any school activities. It was the middle of June and trout fishing was at full throttle. We hatched the bright idea that we would go fishing at one of our favorite "hot spots" called Paine Brook, fish the first afternoon and sleep in the woods that night. Our mothers decided that any school events would be much improved if we weren't there, and off we went.

Reaching Paine Brook and our favorite place on the brook, we set up camp, and went about the business of catching our supper, specifically brook trout rolled in corn meal and fried in salt pork. With full bellies and a beautiful, moonlit June night, we finally stretched out in our sleeping bags for a good night's sleep. The Kid was sleeping between me and the edge of the brook. Being young and not knowing any better, we wrapped our remaining breakfast trout in ferns and placed them in the cold, spring-fed stream. We were fifteen at the time and relatively inexperienced.

Consequently, we gave no thought to the idea that the forest critters might be interested in a meal of trout, at our expense.

The Kid was perhaps the jumpiest person that I know to this day. Virtually anything unexpected would startle him and would make him crazy. Somewhere in the middle of the night, I was jolted out of a sound sleep by his screaming and yelling as though the world was ending. He bolted out of his sleeping bag and took off running through the alders. When he finally stopped, I yelled and asked what the hell was wrong. Between gasps, he said that he had been attacked by bobcats! To calm him down, I added wood to our campfire and lit a lantern. When I questioned him about what made him think that a bobcat had attacked, he explained that at least three bobcats had run across the bottom of his sleeping bag and growled at him.

I was sure that I had the answer and flashed my light on the water where the trout had been. All that remained were a few scattered ferns and one small trout that was bitten in half. The mud on the shore was covered with tracks from a group of raccoons that had smelled out our left-over trout and decided to seize the opportunity. I returned to a peaceful sleep, dreaming of bobcats, raccoons and trout. The Kid stayed awake until daylight.

Eventually, fate and life would take the Kid to Southeast Asia as a marine. Simply dreadful combat experiences forever left their mark on him. We've remained the dearest of friends but health issues prevent him from getting into the woods with me these days. Sixty-three years as pals has slowed us both down, but we have endless memories of one escapade after another, often involving hunting or fishing for one species or another. We reflect on these memories with laughter and reminisce about stories told again and again. And he still insists that they were bobcats!

The other man who has meant so much to my life came along just a few short years after the Kid. David was the exact opposite of my other friend, very deliberate in everything that he did and politically active for most of his life. David and I were the first two members of the world-famous (at least in the West Forks) Wardens Worry Social Club. We both lived in Skowhegan, and we were together regularly and managing numerous days of fishing annually. We made up for lost time with fishing, cribbage (my one and only twenty-nine hand came against David, much to his chagrin), twice-annual trips to the area around the West Forks, camping on the Kennebec at the place that became known as the Cedars.

Three other fishermen who were as nutty as David and me came along, and we became the Wardens Worry Social Club. Our camp became our headquarters for fishing, golf in Jackman, snowshoeing, poker at every opportunity and a constant stream of memories being made. David was an extremely bright man and enjoyed a steady rise as an executive in the oil industry, working for many years for Maine's largest oil company. He loved coming to camp with us so that he could escape from the formality of the oil business.

Over the years, I played a series of practical jokes on David that were carefully planned and never failed to amuse everyone......that is except David. One winter night, three of us were at camp and David somehow must have gotten into some bad whiskey. Early in the evening, the decision was made that David should go to bed. As soon as his head hit the pillow, he was out.

I grabbed a rope and tied one end around his ankle, and the other to his bunk. I covered him up with every spare blanket and sleeping bag that I could find, then filled the wood stove to capacity and opened the damper about half-way. As planned, about midnight David woke, thrashing and flailing in his bed, trying to get out from under all the covers, saying, "Whew, hot, hot, too many covers."

Given the beverages that he'd consumed, he badly needed a trip outside. He took about three steps and hit the end of that rope. When he ran out of rope, there was a hell of a crash when he hit the floor. For some unknown reason, he immediately blamed me and made several references to my ancestors' supposed occupation.

David passed away on August 20th, 2017. As we did when Peter passed, the remaining members of the Wardens Worry

Social Club honored his passing in style. His ashes and his memory have been properly immortalized. Fang, I'll see you on the River someday.

My relationship with Bob Wagg started by accident. My fishing companions (later to become infamous as the "Wardens Worry Social Club") and I were to meet at West Forks and camp on the Kennebec River for a few days of fishing, games of chance, and recreational beverages. Given that I was the first to arrive at our campsite and it was too windy to fish, I visited the famous Sterling Hotel, just across the river. The Sterling is a beautiful old inn that hearkens back to the era of logging and river drives. I've always had suspicions that the hotel was once a "sporting house" for loggers and river men, where alcohol and the company of ladies of questionable virtue were available.

Bob and I struck up a conversation and he asked where I was from. Explaining that I lived in Skowhegan, but was born in Brunswick, Bob immediately perked up and asked my father's name. When I said that my dad was Maurice Ware, his reply was, "Maurice Ware was my best friend!" Thus began a 20+ year relationship that provided me with endless stories about my dad that I never would have known. Bob was an equipment operator by trade, but in his heart he was a trapper and woodsman of considerable note.

Perhaps some of my readers have happened to see a documentary film titled "Dead River Rough Cut". This documentary was produced in the 1990s and was about Bob and his friend, Walter Lane, both of whom were from Brunswick. The film documented their adventures, first as loggers using oxen in the Brunswick area, and later as trappers in the area around Spencer Lake, in the vast woodland between West Forks and Jackman. Walter's rendition of "The Cremation of Sam McGee" is priceless.

Bob and Walter lived a very spartan trapper's life, in a camp that was very near Spencer Lake and the World War II prison camp monument that stands today. During WWII, there actually was a prison camp here where German soldiers were held.

As my relationship with Bob grew, I learned many stories about my dad that somehow, my old man had failed to share. I realized early on that whiskey, aka "recreational beverages," often played a role in their adventures, many of which I'd never heard before. One of the early stories Bob shared was about their annual spring fishing trip to Cheney Pond, located between Jackman and the Quebec border in a very remote area.

Bob and Dad were there with other friends. Dad and one of the others went up the lake to fish one of their "hotspots". When they didn't return, a search party was formed. Bob and the gang arrived at the upper end of Cheney Pond to discover that Dad and Fred had flipped their canoe over, fortunately close to shore, but they were severely hypothermic when Bob and the boys found them. As Bob shared this story with me nearly fifty years after it happened, he said that they took the guys back to the camp and immediately got them out of their wet clothes and built a huge bonfire. Bob's story was that he finally realized how profoundly cold Dad and Fred were when he offered my Dad a drink of whiskey and he refused!

Over the next few years, Lila and I spent many visits to the West Forks enjoying Bob's company. Bob showed us many of the "secret" spots where he and Walter had trapped, fished and hunted. One of my favorites to this day is Bob's "cave" on the shore of a small pond, located a short distance from Spencer Lake. Bob's cave wasn't really a cave, rather it was a cavern formed when the ridge behind it split apart and two pieces of granite the size of a house tumbled down the mountain and piled up together, forming a cavern. In the days when Bob and Walter were tending their trap lines, they would occasionally overnight at the cave, piled up in their bedrolls and with a roaring fire to heat the rocks and keep them warm. Where the two pieces of the ledge came together, a gap was left which formed a natural chimney. This allowed the smoke from the camp fire to funnel its way up and out of the cave.

Among my most cherished memories of Bob centers around our two daughters, Sara and Leslie. Bob dearly loved children and our girls loved him. They were fascinated by his persona and his stories. Bob spent the last few years of his life in the West Forks living in a very small trailer. His mother gave him a very comfortable and much larger mobile home, but after a few weeks Bob swapped it with someone for the smaller one because he had "too goddam much company!"

Bob lived a very simple life and was not necessarily a big advocate of soap and water. By mid-summer, he was usually pretty "ripe" and when we'd take the girls to camp at The Forks, these trips always involved a visit to see Bob. He loved to see the girls and would always give them a big hug. After we'd leave Bob, Sara would always say, "Daddy, he stinks!" But they loved Bob and he loved them.

Bob always used to talk about going down to the Dead River in May, after ice-out, for his annual spring bath. I used to tease Bob by reminding him that, when he hopped into the frigid water of the Dead River and washed his hands, he'd find that pair of mittens that he'd lost in January.

Bob had a very deep-seated dislike of politicians and wealthy people. It took little or no effort whatsoever to get him fired up and ranting about these two groups of people. On the subject of wealthy people, Bob for some reason had singled out the Greek tycoon, Aristotle Onassis. Bob's comment about this fellow was to say that "I'm tellin' ya, nobody ever made that much money without bein' crooked!" On the subject of politicians he'd say, "I ain't votin' for any of em', cause' they're crooked too!" It was always worth the time that it took to sit back and listen to Bob as he ranted and raved. What I'd give to hear him do that again.

Bob always talked about the ice caves near Spencer Lake. He insisted that they were really there and that if you went into the caves in July, you'd find ice still left from the winter. He gave me directions to the caves and assured me that they were easy to find. Two years ago, my fellow members of the Wardens Worry Social Club and I went to look for them. While we didn't find the entrance to the caves, we are sure that we were close because Bob's directions led us to a steep area of exposed ledge which Bob had described. We were short on time that particular day but we are confident that we've found them and will go back soon.

The lives that those woodsmen and women of Bob's and my grandfather's era lived were remarkable in the demands that life and work placed on them, and their stoic acceptance of those demands. They cut and handled every stick of wood that was used to heat their homes and cook their meals. Insulation for those homes was what was called rock wool or plain old sawdust. The river drivers who escorted the pulp down the rivers in the spring didn't have Gore-Tex or Thinsulate. They had rubber boots at best. I remember my uncle describing how, when the cook and his cookee would show up with the horse-drawn wagons or sleds with the hot lunches, the river drivers would think nothing of wading through the icy water to get to the other shore where a hot meal waited.

I still have my grandfather's lunch box which looks like a submarine. The top is hollow and has a large, round lid. They'd put hot soup in the lid, which served to keep the sandwiches, biscuits and handfuls of cookies in the lower part from freezing. All this and hot tea, strong enough to melt a spoon, as Gramp described it.

I've heard people say that life in those days was simpler. It may have been that, but it damn sure wasn't easier. Bob and those of his era were remarkable people, and as tough as boiled owls.

Bob, rest in peace. You were part of a disappearing breed; Maine will never see your like again.

In my lifetime, I have had the privilege of enjoying many, many outhouses. In the process of galloping all over two continents, I have visited outhouses of every size, shape and with widely varying levels of comfort, to say nothing of décor.

I've discovered that one's enjoyment of an outhouse is directly related to one's need to be there in the first place. Décor, protection from the weather, and overall comfort share a confirmed second place to functionality. Outhouses often serve a variety of purposes, depending on circumstances.

I was guiding caribou hunters once in the area of Quebec's Delay River for an outfitter whose hunts we were marketing. The caribou migration was in full throttle, and the animals were moving by the tent camp regularly day and night. One morning, as my hunters and I were preparing to leave, one of the hunters that I was guiding announced that he needed to visit one of the outhouses before we climbed into the boats and left for the day's hunt. He started to lay his rifle down before he headed to the facilities and I reminded him that we had caribou passing the camps often in order to cross the lake so that they could migrate further. I mentioned that it would be too bad to be in the outhouse and see the bull of a lifetime stroll by and have no weapon within reach.

As we watched him walk to the outhouse, I looked up at the top of the ridge behind the camps and sure enough, a group of bachelor bulls came over the top. I asked my hunters to keep down and said, "Watch this!"

The hunter was in the outhouse with the door closed as several of these bulls, including one absolutely spectacular bull, walked by the outhouse at about thirty yards. All remained quiet and we wondered if he had become so absorbed in the task at hand that he hadn't seen the bulls.

All of a sudden, the outhouse door flew open with a bang and out jumped my hunter, gun in hand and his pants around his ankles!

It goes without saying that the trophy bull stopped and looked like he'd lost his mind. There was a moment of total silence, followed by a loud bang as our hunter shot the bull. The other bulls stopped as if they'd never seen anything like this. There were several other bulls in this group that were certainly "shooters," but the rest of us were so doubled over with laughter, that we couldn't even get the guns up. Trust me, many pictures were taken.

Outhouses range in quality and convenience from something as simple as a "cat hole" in the woods, tastefully located downwind from the campsite. The outhouse that we have at our camp in West Forks (not to be confused or compared with The Forks) is a beauty. When we first bought the camp, forever after known as the headquarters of the Wardens Worry Social Club, there were five members of our club.

Two of the fellows were contractors and one of them had just done a major kitchen renovation for a wealthy Portland doctor. As it turned out, the doctor had chosen what was at the time the best Formica money could buy for his kitchen counter tops. David had finished the job with some leftover sheets of this material and he turned those leftovers into what we have always described as "the finest shithouse north of the Mason-Dixon Line."

We have a beautiful commode made from the Formica, complete with a vent stack, coffee cans for toilet paper storage and the obligatory copies of LL Bean's catalogs. We also have a Sterno heater for those really cold mornings. Early each morning, a deck of cards is produced and we cut the cards to see who gets the dubious distinction of making the first trip to our little home away from home to melt the frost off the seat.

Lila and I flew via float-plane into a remote Maine lake for several years. The pilot would drop us and our gear off and return in a week. Given that we were at a primitive campsite, outhouses were non-existent. On our first trip to this lake, ever the gentleman, I was concerned for Lila's comfort and privacy. Not only did

I bring a chain saw, I also brought a toilet seat! I made a private, amazingly plush toilet that provided a scenic view of the lake, and yet was a discreet distance from our camp and the Appalachian Trail. Nothing was too good for my fiancé.

One morning, as Lila was frying bacon, I decided to make a quick trip to our facilities. As I sat there blissfully enjoying the scenery, I discovered that I had company. There I was, sitting and minding my own business and suddenly I was not alone. A large bear, who could not have cared less about me but was extremely interested in the bacon that Lila was cooking, strolled by me within 50 feet. I didn't know whether or not to sit still or go rescue her from the bear. The first decision that I made was to pull my pants up in case he came my way, making the assumption that I couldn't run very fast with my pants around my ankles. Having made myself presentable, I yelled "Hey" to the bear. Taking one look at me he made for parts unknown very quickly. I am certain that, to this day, this bear is still thinking, "What in the hell was that?"

Outhouses were usually a carefully-designed part of any household in years gone by. Lila's grandmother had a beautiful old New England farmhouse with, what was often the case with these old farms, an attached woodshed that held the year's supply of firewood for cook stoves and fireplaces. Usually, these wood-sheds were between the house and the barn where the livestock was housed. Woodsheds were often where the family outhouse was located. Toilet paper was not always available and this is where the Sears Roebuck catalog wound up.

For obvious reasons, these outhouses were usually on an out-side wall of the barn or woodshed. This also meant that the back wall of the outhouse faced a long field or pasture. I'll leave it to you to guess how much velocity a cold February wind could generate as it made its way across the field to the outhouse. Trips to these outhouses were usually very brief and to the point. This was not the time for procrastination.

I have spent countless hours sitting in outhouses in many states and provinces. One of my most enjoyable pastimes is sitting in an outhouse, listening to the world around me as it wakes up. I used to use an outhouse located in a bush camp on a very remote lake in Quebec. Other than the obvious intent, I could have sat there for hours, listening to the wind, seeing the water lap the shoreline, and watching Mother Nature as she went about her early-morning chores.

Outhouses are structures to be cherished, kept functional and not to be taken for granted. Lastly, every now and then, somebody has to get out the long-handled spade and shovel out the debris under the building. Get that deck of cards out and keep your fingers crossed! Yuuk!

The Crazy Frenchman

In 1986, Lila and I made our first-ever trip to the interior of Quebec to the Broadback River Fishing Camps (BRFC). This trip was very special because the purpose was to fly fish for legitimately BIG brook trout. In those days, a trophy at the Broadback was any brookie over five pounds. The previous year, we'd had friends fish at the BRFC with great success and big trout caught. So in August of 1986, Lila and I drove to the village of Chibougamau (say that fast 3 times!), overnighted there and flew via DeHaviland Beaver float plane to the camps.

Our host was a gentleman named Richard Demers. Our week with Richard at the BRFC was fantastic for several reasons. First is the fact that we both caught biggest brook trout that we'd ever seen, much less been able to battle on a fly rod. Tact and diplomacy forces me to admit that Lila's trout, at six pounds, four ounces, was larger than my puny five-pounder. But, we also caught walleye, which for my money is the very best table fish short of a ten inch brookie, anywhere. And, with Northern pike filling out our week's success, we just had the time of our lives.

Coincidentally, at this point in my life I needed to make a career change. After having a fantastic visit to the BRFC and getting to know Richard, we came home, thought about our experience and wondered if there was an opportunity for us to start our own business.

So one evening the following October, fueled by a couple of glasses of a great Cabernet, we called Richard and explained that we had an "idea." We were sure that we could sell enough fishing business for him annually so that we could come and fish for a week for free. We discussed the particulars of our idea and asked Richard what he thought. It took him about three seconds to say with his French accent, "What da hell, I done dumber t'ings!"

With Richard's words, Fins and Furs Adventures was born. More later on about our business ventures, but at that moment we were in the fishing business, just as if we really knew what we were doing. Our business relationship with Richard lasted for twelve years, until he sold the business. Additionally, and very quickly, Richard became one of our very dearest friends as our business and personal relationships grew.

Richard had a bit of a wild streak and loved to have a good time. He was about as good as anyone that we've ever met at making the most out of life. He was one of those people who could do anything ("anyt'ing" in his words) with his hands. We learned so many things from Richard, including how NOT to run a fishing lodge. I say that with a great amount of affection, because Richard sometimes could be his own worst enemy. However, he taught us the value of catch and release practices, especially when those giant trout, which he referred to as his "babies," were involved. He taught us to fillet pike and walleye and to skin a trophy trout when preparing it for taxidermy.

Richard was not the world's most happy person when he first arose in the morning. Naturally, once I figured this out, I stood outside his bedroom window early one morning and played a song called "The Wildwood Flower" on my harmonica. He wouldn't speak to me until about 11:00 a.m. that day.

As time passed, Richard, Lila and I made a career out of playing practical jokes on each other, or anyone else that was foolish enough to be in range. One year we took a couple of our friends to the BRFC with us. We convinced our friend to volunteer to be the best man at a wedding ceremony, with Richard as the groom. What we "forgot" to tell Richard was that his bride was an inflatable sex doll that came from a porn shop in Lewiston. I suspect that it goes without saying that a liberal amount of recreational beverages were in use that day.

On another occasion, Lila and I happened to be the only ones staying in Richard's largest camp, which was a beautiful log cabin that slept six people. Unbeknownst to us, Richard had gotten his hands on an "Ah Ooga" horn out of an old Ford tractor. While we were fishing that afternoon, Richard snuck into our camp and hid the horn under Lila's bed, then had run the wires out through a gap in the logs to a battery. He went to great lengths to be sure that all the other dozen or so of our customers who were in camp with us knew about this.

Lila and I announced that we were calling it a day. We have always made a habit when we are on these trips to lie in her bed or mine for a while and talk about our day. As soon as we were in our camp, Richard gathered everyone else in the camp yard. After giving us time to get into bed, he connected the wires on the battery. Unfortunately, the switch on the horn was stuck and so it just made a buzzing noise that no one outside the camp could hear, but we sure could. When the horn didn't go off, Richard ran in through the door with a spotlight and flashed it on us lying there in the same bunk in complete innocence. When he saw us lying there together, he went back to the door and yelled to the crowd, "De're bot' in de same bed!"

Another of Richard's many lessons was the art of a beer-batter fish fry. We have so many memories of shore lunches on the shores of Lac Assinica, which are the headwaters of the Broadback River. Nothing is much better than fresh-caught walleye, cooked in oil or lard (guaranteed to jump your cholesterol level by two or three times), with fried potatoes, home-made bread in Ginette's outdoor baking oven, all washed down with hot, strong black tea. As I recall, we preceded the hot tea with the beer which was of course required to make the batter.

Richard Demers was instrumental in our lives because he was the spark that gave us the idea of launching Fins and Furs Adventures.

We lost Richard to cancer in May of 2003. It was for both Lila and me like losing a big brother. The last time we saw him was in August of 2002, when we returned to Montreal after having been with a group of our caribou hunters on the Leaf River of northern Quebec. We had seen him at the hotel on the way up, and when we returned to the hotel from the hunt, he was there, waiting for us.

Richard was in his late sixties then and took great pride in, and was happy to remind me, that even at his age he had not one gray hair. Richard, especially when he had been tipping the Gran Marnier Cognac, always referred to me with his Quebec accent as his "little brudder." I carry those words on my chest, over my heart, to this day. Those spectacular days on the Broadback were simply priceless.

Rest in peace my friend, you taught us things that have been a part of our approach to life in general and our business in particular, to this day.

One September evening in the early eighties on the banks of the Kennebec River a mile or so above the village of West Forks, five men stood around a campfire after a day of fishing in the area. Originally there were just two of us. David and I knew each other from high school and had renewed our friendship after not seeing much of each other for six or so years. Over the years, three other men joined our group for fishing, poker, cribbage, fantastic meals and various types of "recreational beverages." We quickly grew very close, making a spring and fall fishing adventure annually. As our friendship moved along, I took it upon myself to come up with a name for our group. Taking this as a serious responsibility, I gave the matter much thought and came up with, and then soon discarded, various titles for our group of five.

I am a fan of movies in the western genre, those starring John Wayne, Jimmy Stewart and Henry Fonda in particular. One of my favorites was a movie titled the Cheyenne Social Club. In this movie, Jimmy Stewart had somehow inherited a house of ill repute, named the Cheyenne Social Club. I loved the movie and the title but realized that for it to work for us, it needed an outdoors-related connotation.

Consequently, as we stood around the campfire that September evening, without anyone knowing what was coming, I said, "Gentlemen, I want to propose a toast." For our group someone proposing a toast was not only commonplace, we had shown a propensity to toast damn near anything. Trout, moose, water, omelets, rocks in the river, very little was off the table when it came to subjects for a toast.

That evening, we raised our glasses as I said; "To the five members of the Wardens Worry Social Club (by the way, a Wardens Worry is a streamer fly, used for trout), good times and good grub. Wet flies and wet feet, the rises that we missed and some of 'em we didn't. I dedicate this, our inaugural toast, to the perpetuation of our trips together forever."

David and I were the two original members of this auspicious group. For some reason that neither of us could ever remember, David and I always had called each other Fang. Thinking that the newest members of the group needed a nickname, Peter soon became Macklin, after a character in a John Wayne movie. Jim and Kirk became Shortlegs and Eagle, due to Jim's short stature and Kirk's blonde hair.

The very next year, the group found and purchased, a camp six miles north of West Forks. There was immediately a serious uptick in the number of weekends spent at camp, including remodeling the entire interior of the camp, building a woodshed, and many other projects. Most of these projects were conducted with loads of ribald humor, cocktails on our newly-made deck, and perhaps most importantly, the installation of a new outhouse.

Kirk was at this time employed by the State of Maine as the supervisor of a department that was called the Surplus Property Dept. The same summer that we bought the camp, Kirk touched base with all of us saying, "Hey, I have found a new shithouse for the camp." It seems as though he'd gotten his hands on a surplus building that would fit our needs perfectly. With very little planning and a complete lack of common sense, we went to Kirk's office, jacked up our brand spankin' new outhouse, put it on a trailer and away we went.

Installing the outhouse was preceded by digging a pit (we dug until we hit bedrock, knowing our group as we did), then carefully installing our little home away from home over the pit. A necessary part of all this was the installation ceremony, which included many toasts and copious amounts of various spirits. If my memory is correct, there is still an empty bottle of champagne at the bottom of the pit. One simply does not install a new outhouse at camp without the appropriate ceremonial moments.

To this day, this little building which somehow came to be christened as "The Finest Shithouse North of the Mason-Dixon Line" stands ready to answer the call of nature. In cold weather, each morning, we cut the cards to see who goes first to melt the ice from the seat.

Years passed and a seemingly endless series of memories continued. We patronized our camp all year-round. Our major winter event became what was known as the WWSC rabbit hunt. This was a major fundraising event for the WWSC. One of the most prestigious events during the rabbit hunt weekend was to present the Sportsman of the Year award. Annually, this honor was bestowed on some unlucky person who was foolish enough to actually attend this soiree. Gifts and eloquent descriptions of the recipient's outdoor prowess, or the lack thereof, were described in great detail. These descriptions were usually at the expense of the "lucky" honoree. None of us can recall for sure, but we think that one year, somebody actually brought a gun!

The common thread in every visit to camp was working on the camp, fishing and hunting, endless funny moments, practical jokes on each other and fantastic meals. Four of the five members of the WWSC loved to cook, with Fang often taking the lead. His fabulous meals served at camp were delicious and featured roast prime rib, Cornish game hens, and homemade breads that were out of this world. However, very little credit was ever extended to Fang. It was too good an opportunity to give him the business about his cooking.

When we finally realized that we couldn't possibly eat three meals a day, we smartened up and rather than an early breakfast a late morning brunch became a success. This gave us time to get on the water someplace, either on the local rivers, the Kennebec and/or the Dead, or to a local pond. We would then head back to camp for another sumptuous meal that we'd rave about, like it was the first time that we ever ate eggs, Carroll's biscuits and home fries. These repasts were usually accompanied by screwdrivers, with fresh orange juice.

As is always the case with things like this, Father Time made his presence known. After nine years when we had made enough memories for several lifetimes, he took his toll. In the spring of 1993, we lost Peter. This was a huge blow to all of us. David said it best when he stated that while he had expected to outlive his parents, he'd never expected to lose one of his "pals."

Nearly twenty-five years later, on August 7, 2017, we lost David. He and I had been as brothers for most of the last fifty years. Today, Kirk, Jim and I are the surviving members of the Wardens Worry Social Club. Little did any of us realize what that evening by the fire, on the banks of the Kennebec would come to. The years have taught me how precious the friendships that we forge are and despite the loss of two of our companions, that life goes forward, as they would have wanted.

I have been so blessed to have been a part of this group of men who came together because of a love of the Maine woods. Our travels have taken us to adventures like chasing walleyes and trout in Quebec and a lifetime of moments in the Maine woods together stuffed into a painfully short fifty years. To this day, I have the luxury of allowing my mind to drift back over those years and finding that I laugh about those times over and over, as though I was reliving them for the first time.

Having these men in my life has reminded me how fortunate I have been to have had them in my life. They helped me discover that men have places that they call "camp," but it often is a destination and not a structure.

Rest in peace, my crazy friends, I'll see you on the River.

Registered Maine Guides are among the most recognized guides anywhere in the world. Our history goes back to the late eighteen hundreds and even earlier. I read a book once about Benedict Arnold's ill-fated journey up the Kennebec River. He made his way through the interior of western Maine on his way to attack the British at Quebec City. During his ordeal up through Maine, he apparently had Native Americans as guides. Kenneth Roberts' book "Arundel" documents this fact.

The first "boom" for Maine's guiding industry came when sporting camps began to open at various locations in Maine. The Moosehead Lake area was a big part of this era, as was eastern Maine, the Kennebec and Dead Rivers, and famously, Rangeley. It's interesting to note that in the late eighteen hundreds the largest brook trout being caught anywhere in the world were being caught in the Rangeley area. There are almost unlimited numbers of photos and stories of guides working out of the big hotels in Rangeley and the huge brook trout that were taken. Unfortunately, most of the time with no thought of conservation of the species at hand. A common way to display these magnificent, but very dead, trout was to lay the day's catch across the keel of a canoe with guides and "sports" included.

Over the last thirty-five or so years, Lila and I have been fortunate to own a business that has taken us all over two continents and to many lodges. In the course of all this we've come into contact with many guides. Most of them were fantastic people and very skilled at the trade. They were memorable for any of several reasons.

Our first real experience with a guide was during our initial trip to the Broadback River Fishing Camps. The BRFC would be the first outfitter that we took on as a client when we opened Fins and Furs Adventures. Our guide for that first trip to the

Broadback was the owner of the BRFC, Richard Demers. Richard's father, Rene, was somewhat of a legend in the outfitting industry in Quebec and first opened the camps in the early seventies. He passed away soon after and Richard took over the operation of the camps.

As we got off the Otter floatplane, Richard was there to greet us and one of our first questions after finishing introductions was "How's the fishing been?" Richard's reply became one of the first things that we admired about him. He said, "If you ask a question at the BRFC, you get an honest answer. The fishing has been lousy for a week!" Fortunately, the trout Gods smiled on us that day because that very afternoon things turned around and the big brookies began to cooperate.

We had been on the river for less than two hours with Richard when Lila hooked and landed the biggest brook trout we'd ever seen. Richard weighed the trout at six pounds, four ounces and we were stunned. It is worth mentioning that for the rest of our week with Richard the biggest trout that I could find was a puny five pounds.

One of the things that became very apparent early in the week with Richard was that he possessed an intimate knowledge of the river and his "babies" as he referred to the trophy trout there. He also had a rather unusual approach to his attention to Lila and me as we fished. He knew every rock and riffle in that river and didn't see much sense in standing there looking over our shoulders, so he'd grab a fast nap.

The second morning, we were at what he called Number 3 Pool, and I looked around to ask our guide something. There was Richard stretched out on the rocks and apparently sound asleep. It turned out that he was merely relaxing, getting what he called his "river nap." At the first hint that we'd spotted or hooked a fish he was on his feet in a heartbeat ready to help if needed. Richard was as knowledgeable about his fishery as any guide that we have worked with and we've had a ton of them.

Over the many years that we were associated with Richard and the BRFC, we had several different guides with varying levels of skill and ambition. One year, we had a twenty-something young man whose name escapes me, but we'll call him Sleepy. We chose this nickname for him because to say that Sleepy's guiding skills and his experience left a lot to be desired was an understatement of epic proportions. When Richard stretched out on the rocks he was listening and watching every second. When Sleepy lay down he'd be snoring within minutes. We lost a few fish that week because he'd been sleeping. By the time he got to us it was too late.

Sleepy also had little boat operation experience and that gave us some anxious moments on the river, too. After three days of Sleepy, we brought all this to Richard's attention and Sleepy was on the next plane out. When he came to say good bye to us, his gratuity was a five dollar bill (Canadian funds) that I tucked in his pocket. At that he was over-tipped substantially.

I have mentioned that my mother and her family all came from Flagstaff and that Gramp operated Spring Lake Camps. One of the most noted guides at those camps was a fellow named Rube Dexter. Rube was a very well-known fixture at the camps and in the entire area. One fall during deer season Rube's customers were two bankers from Ohio who'd travelled nearly two weeks via train to get there. Their plan was to spend three weeks at Spring Lake deer hunting with Rube.

Gramp managed the camps and my Uncle Ken happened to be there hunting with his brother, Bob. The bankers had been there nearly two weeks and had not had a single chance at a big buck. The first morning that Uncle Ken was there hunting, he shot a sixteen-point buck that weighed substantially over two hundred pounds. As Uncle Ken was field-dressing the buck, Rube and the boys came along. The bankers were not just a little unhappy that they'd been there two weeks and Uncle Ken had been there a couple of hours and had already taken this magnificent buck. The bankers were expressing their disappointment to Rube who, after listening to their comments, finally said, "Well, don't ya know them ole bucks will do somethin' stupid ever' once in a while?"

Another Rube story involves the chef at Spring Lake. This Italian chef was rather hot tempered, and as it happened, Rube and the chef detested each other. The chef was continually trying to make Rube look foolish.

There was a very substantial vegetable garden at the camps producing fresh fare for the camp guests. The chef complained to Rube that there was a huge woodchuck destroying the fruits of the garden. One morning about 5:00 a.m., the chef woke Rube out of a sound sleep asking him to shoot the critter in the garden. Rube's gun of choice was an old Winchester .38-55. The garden was more than 100 yards from the door of the kitchen which made the woodchuck tough to see and a very difficult shot. Rube went to the door, looked carefully down the rifle barrel, squeezed the trigger and shot the woodchuck in the head. Without a word he turned and went back to bed. The chef went out and grabbed the woodchuck carcass and hid it.

The next morning the chef went to the garden propped the woodchuck up with a couple of small sticks so it seemed a second animal had appeared. One of the chef's pleasures in life was having an excuse to wake Rube early. He roused Rube, telling him that there was a second woodchuck in the garden. Rube appeared shortly with his gun and went to the door (Rube was famous for his spectacular eyesight). Rube loaded the gun, raised it and everyone waited for the bang as the gun went off. Rube instead lowered the rifle, gave the chef a look that would have killed and said, "I shot that un' yestiddy."

Lila has on many occasions over the last forty years had the dubious distinction of having me as her guide. One beautiful July day about 30 years ago, I got the bright idea that we should drive to The Forks, leave our vehicle at the ball field, and hike a couple of miles up the Kennebec to a beautiful run of water with a great pool at the tail-out called Stand-Up Rips.

My great plan was that, because the weather forecast was calling for overnight temperatures in the 70s, we wouldn't need a sleeping bag. We'd travel light, sleep in a small two-person tent and carry what we needed to cook a couple of trout the next morning. I brought a tea kettle, cast-iron skillet, biscuits, salt pork and corn meal. Fresh trout, hot tea and biscuits, cooked on an open fire right beside the water are a classic Maine Guide presentation. Hey, we're talkin' romance here!

As the best-laid plans of mice and men sometimes go, the weatherman pulled a fast one and by midnight, the temperature had dropped into the thirties. Suffice to say that neither of us got much, if any, sleep that night. Most of my nocturnal activities that night were following Lila's strict orders to keep the fire going. I had great plans for a romantic evening beside the fire, sipping wine and listening to the river as it made its way past us. The only things that I heard were threats against my well-being if I didn't keep the fire roaring.

By the way, breakfast was only hot tea and reheated biscuits, because the trout apparently didn't care much for the cool weather either.

At one time a number of years ago, Lila and I sold elk and mule deer hunts for a guide in Montana. As was our policy, we went to Montana and spent a week hunting with him before we agreed to market his business. Our accommodations on this hunt ranged from truly quaint and unique, to primitive and then some.

For the first three days of the hunt, we traveled via horseback (as usual, I fell off the horse), and stayed in tent camps. My horse was named Scotchy and Lila's steed was Eugene. We were rookies at horseback riding but both of our mounts were well trail-broken and very docile. However, Eugene liked to be in front and so several times a day, with no noticeable provocation, he'd take it upon himself to run by all the other horses and get in front. This seemed to irritate our outfitter and we quickly discovered that they use the same curse words in Montana that we do in Maine.

My horse, Scotchy was happy just to plod along and was happiest when we were stopped. It soon became clear that there was something that happened to him internally when he was not walking. The second that we pulled up, old Scotchy would begin to fart. I don't mean a brief burst of gas, I mean long, drawn out eruptions that lasted for ten or fifteen seconds. I have always thought that I was pretty proficient when it comes to passing gas, but I soon learned that I was in the presence of greatness! After the first morning, Lila refused to ride behind me; guess I couldn't blame her.

The tent camp that we stayed in was at about eight thousand feet above sea level. This meant several things and perhaps the most notable was that it was very cold. Our sleeping tent was comfortable with sleeping pads, extra sleeping bags and a wood stove with plenty of wood. But the hedgehog in the wood pile was that the stove would not hold enough wood to last all night. We'd set an alarm clock for midnight and then again at four a.m. I, being the dutiful and loyal husband, was always the one who graciously volunteered to crawl out of our zipped together sleeping bags to fill the stove.

We discovered that cold at 8,000 feet in the Beaverhead National Forest was a very dry cold, much different from Maine. We had, naturally, an outhouse for a toilet and I learned that the definition of a real gentleman is that he is the one who makes the first trip to the outhouse in the morning to melt the frost off the seat. It was so cold that when we'd use our tin coffee cups to brush our teeth in the before-dawn cold, the water in the cup would start to freeze before we were done brushing.

When we came out of the mountains after the first few days, the plan was for us to hunt at lower altitudes as the cold had pushed the elk and deer down into lower forests. We moved to a beautiful and old community called Wise River. Many of the buildings there were very old and much as they were when built.

We stayed at a place called the Wise River Club. The original structure dated back to the mid-eighteen hundreds and was originally a saloon. There were lots of artifacts and old photos of days long gone. The bar was the original bar that had always been there. Cigar burns and a brass rail that showed the wear of boots placed on it for a hundred years made it even more unique. All the beds in the rooms were made from Lodge pole Pine, put together by a local craftsman.

We spent several evenings in the bar and half expected a gunfight to break out anytime. We met an assortment of true western characters. It was frequented by loggers, rodeo riders, and many of the locals who were just wonderful people.

On our next to last evening there a friend of our outfitter, who was also a guide, walked in, hobbling around with a cast on one ankle. It turned out that he was a bull rider on the professional bull riding circuit. He'd been tossed from a bull and broken his right ankle. The stories of his bull-riding career just rolled out of him. We kept buying the beers and he kept talking. As the evening broke up everyone agreed to meet up the next night, our last one there, for more stories.

When we returned to the Wise River Club after our last day of hunting, we were told that the cowboy had gotten a phone call. Somebody called, offering him a chance to ride bulls in a big-money rodeo in Las Vegas, and he'd left. When we asked how he'd ride bulls with a cast on one ankle, they said that he found a hacksaw, sawed the cast off, jumped in his truck and headed for Las Vegas!

A more humorous moment occurred at another caribou camp that was operated by the first caribou outfitter we had ever worked with. While the hunting and the fishing were quite good, the camps left a little to be desired as did the camp manager/guide. The manager was a native of Quebec and supposedly only spoke very broken English. I speak what I've always referred to as "fishing camp French," which means my entire command of the French language is to ask what time it is and "where's the bathroom?" Any ability to communicate with the manager, whom the group named "Pepi", was very limited and no one could pronounce his actual name in French.

The Quebec caribou are migratory animals, meaning that as the summer winds down, the herds migrate from their summer ground, on the Ungava Peninsula, south to the areas where they will spend the winter, birth their calves in the spring and then begin their trek north again.

One of the set-in-stone rules of caribou outfitting is that if the hunting area near the camps has no animals close by, the outfitter brings in a floatplane to fly hunters out for the day to an area where there are caribou. This allows the hunters to harvest their animals and then return to the camps. On arriving at camp this particular trip, there were no caribou close to camp. After a day and a half of no caribou, the group began to pressure Pepi to bring in a plane to fly the hunters out. His reply was "tomorrow, tomorrow." On the third day, the answer was again, "Tomorrow." It is worth mentioning that six of these hunters were from Millinocket, Maine, and worked in the huge paper mill that existed there at that time. They were great guys but a little "rough" on the outside. On day four, the ringleader of this bunch went to Pepi and demanded he bring a plane in, but sure enough, Pepi's reply was as before, "Tomorrow."

The ringleader told Pepi in very graphic terms that if there wasn't a plane in by 9:00 a.m. the following day, they would burn to the ground the cabin that Pepi slept in!

At seven the next morning, Pepi was asked about the plane and when it would arrive. Pepi shrugged and raised his hands, palm up, as if to say he didn't know, and he went to the kitchen camp for coffee. Pepi emerged from the kitchen with a cup of coffee to see that the boys were gathering driftwood and piling it around his camp! The ringleader looked at Pepi and said, "Ya got two hours and then we're touchin' her off!" Pepi panicked, ran for the radio and frantically called the float plane base, screaming into the radio, likely to plead for a plane before his camp was reduced to ashes. At 9:00 a.m. sharp, the boys, true to their word, were gathering up tinder and small sticks and were about ready to "touch her off," when we heard to familiar roar of the Otter just clearing the ridge across the lake. Fortunately for Pepi, they flew the hunters out, everyone filled their two caribou tags (one hunter also took a very large bear) and things calmed down. But the boys left the driftwood piled around Pepi's camp for the rest of the week, and anything that they wanted, they got. All of a sudden on that memorable day, Pepi's English also got a lot better.

Trust me, though, when I say that even though Lila and I feel entirely comfortable afield or on the waters, we don't want to waste time searching for productive spots when we travel to new locations. We always hire a qualified guide.

I was guiding at one of Maine's oldest and best known sporting camps many years ago. On Sunday afternoon when the new group of guests rolled in, one of them, who had no idea if I was to be his guide or not, started firing questions about all the wild birds and game he expected to see. Over the next few days, when the guides were in the crew's dining area behind the kitchen, this guy would come out and regale us with his sightings of birds and mammals. A couple of things became apparent quite quickly: first, he considered himself to be a wildlife expert and second, he wanted to be sure that everyone in camp knew it. We were pretty sure that, like most blowhards, he would eventually make himself look like the village idiot.

It took a couple of days but one evening, we were all sitting around the fire pit in front of the lodge talking about the day and our successes, or lack thereof. Before long, in rolls Mr. Wildlife Expert, raving about all the game that he'd seen. By this time all the guides were on to him and so we just let him ramble on, sure that he'd make a gaffe sooner or later.

Finally, one of us asked him which wild game had he seen the most of on the way back to the camps that evening? Without thinking, he blurted out his answer, "I am telling you, we must have seen at least two dozen horseshoe hares." He obviously had meant to say *snow*shoe hares, which are correctly called varying hares because they change from brown during the summer to white in winter. But, he no sooner got the words out of his mouth than we all broke into hysterical laughter. He spun on the heel of his boot, went to his cabin and for the rest of the week, was very subdued and kept his wildlife analysis to himself.

During the ten or so years that Lila and I guided at and managed Bosebuck Mountain Camps west of Rangeley on Aziscohos Lake, we had a fellow who was cut from the same cloth. His self-proclaimed prowess centered on fishing. He was a lake fisherman who spent his days trolling streamers and various types of lures, up and down Aziscohos Lake. Each day, during the evening meal, he'd regale anyone who would listen in the dining room about all the trout and salmon that he'd released that day. Oddly enough, he never had any pictures ("no pictures, I release 'em right away") and the only trout that he brought were smaller fish that barely met the slot limit requirements.

On one particular evening, he crowed about catching several big brook trout and landlocked salmon. Having had as much of him as everyone else, I asked him what he had used for a lure and his reply was, "Boy, I caught 'em all on a Moose Lip Wobbler!" Sad for him but the jig was up. In his infinite wisdom, he was trying to say Moose*look* Wobbler, which is a very well-known lure that has been a favorite of spin fishermen for decades. At that point his credibility immediately reached an all-time low.

Over the many years that I, and for the last 40 years Lila and I, have roamed all over Robin Hood's barn, we have heard and seen many humorous (most of them) exchanges between guides and their customers. We marketed trophy brook trout and landlocked salmon for fly fishermen at Riverkeep Lodge in Labrador. On my first visit there, I had the honor of being guided by a true gentleman named Horace Goudie.

Horace, his father, and uncles were Labrador legends in the trapping, hunting and fishing world. Theirs was a difficult, demanding and dangerous lifestyle. These pioneers traveled by boat or canoe up the famed Churchill River and to the interior of Labrador and beyond to the McKenzie River. For me to have had the privilege of being guided by Horace for a week was one of the highlights of my career.

Horace was the head guide of the lodge on the Atikonak River. While I was there with Horace, there was another gent in camp who was from America's midwest. He owned a major corporation that made lawn mowers and tractors. He was very wealthy and loved to brag about his money and all the remote and exclusive locations that he had fished. He was also an egomaniac of epic proportions. He loved to sit around the lodge during supper and fire questions at the guides using his well-practiced "one-upmanship." Horace was by far too smart, too experienced, and too wise to get sucked into a debate with this horse's patoot.

One evening at supper, Horace put him completely in his place and everyone except the loudmouth loved it. Remember this was the early nineties and before the advent of cell and satellite phones. Our only contact with the outside world was by radio communication and then only at specific times of the day. This fellow took great pleasure in trying to put the guides on the spot by asking questions that supposedly only he knew the answer to.

During one evening meal, Loudmouth said in his usual demanding tone, "Horace, what's the weather gonna' be tomorrow?" Horace had just picked up a small piece of roast beef with his fork, and, without ever taking his eyes from his food, said in his usual soft voice, "When the sun goes down it'll be dark and it'll stay that way 'til mornin'."

There was a second or two of silence at the table and then everyone except Loudmouth burst into laughter and gave Horace a round of applause. From that moment on for the rest of the week, old what's-his-name had his hat in his hand.

During my time with Horace at Riverkeep Lodge, I quickly developed a huge amount of respect for him. I was in awe of him and the last thing that I wanted to do was make myself look foolish. All week long I was extremely careful to not put my foot in my mouth, or to show my inexperience.

One beautiful July day, Horace and I were in a twenty-foot square-stern canoe heading up the river to meet everyone else for lunch. The shore lunch spot was located on a picturesque gravel point, where the river dumps out of Atikonak Lake. We'd had a great morning, with some very large brook trout and landlocked salmon caught and released.

As we made our way up the river, we could just see the point and Horace said, with his Labrador accent, "The byes is on the pint." I didn't understand him and asked what he'd said. Again, the answer was, "The byes is on the pint." Without a clue what he'd said, but determined to not look like a rookie, I said, "Oh."

We continued to motor up the river and I kept repeating to myself, "The byes is on the pint?" I had about given up when I looked upriver towards the point and saw the other boats and the smoke from the campfire. All at once, the light came on as I realized that what Horace was saying was, "The boys are on the point!"

About a year before he died, I visited Horace in Goose Bay at the nursing home where he was staying. When I told him this story, he laughed and laughed. Horace was one of those once-in-a-lifetime people. I was so incredibly privileged to have known him and call him my friend.

Any time you are in the Maine woods, anything can and usually does happen. I was up in the Maine North Woods at a sporting camp and we had a group of four couples coming for three days of fishing. One couple was the son and daughter of the other couples and they had just gotten married somewhere down on Maine's coast. The plan was that a float plane would pick them up in Bangor and fly them, two at a time, to the camps.

I was to be one of the guides for this group, and when the two ladies stepped off the plane almost immediately they asked if I could take them for a ride to see if we could spot some wildlife. One of the ladies was a photographer of some note and had a very high-tech Minolta camera with all the bells and whistles. We left the camps and I took them on several gravel roads where we could usually get some level of cooperation from the critters. As we rode along the lady sitting next to me in the front seat of my truck asked if I thought that we'd see any moose. I assured her that finding moose was at least typically an easy task but with wildlife, one never knows.

In about fifteen minutes lo and behold, the "Chamber of Commerce" bull moose stepped out into the road and stood there while the ladies had all the photo ops that they wished. We saw two or three deer soon afterwards and as we were rounding a corner in the dirt road, the same lady who asked about the moose, said, "Do you think that we'll see a bear?"

Before I could get my mouth open, a sow with twin cubs stepped into the road about two hundred feet ahead of us. From the time that she asked about bear, it wasn't three seconds and there they were. Momma huffed at the cubs and sent them up a big rock maple that stood on the edge of the road, and then she stepped into the thick woods at the edge of the road. The gal asked if she could get out for more pictures and I told her no, but to pass me her camera and I'd stand up in the door of the truck without ever putting my feet on the ground. I snapped five or six photos and I could hear Momma huffing and puffing and popping her jaws, making it abundantly clear that she'd had about all of this that she wanted. I stepped back into the truck and we promptly left.

An odd sequel to this sighting was about six or seven months later, I saw one of the pictures that I had taken in a photography magazine with the woman's name in the credits. However, it was not a big deal to me—the lady had sent me a copy of the photo, as promised. Incidentally, that first evening at the camps, the wedding party produced not one but TWO bottles of Dom Perignon champagne. Trust me when I say that Boone's Farm will never be confused with Dom Perignon.

The last of my "did they really say that" moments involved a group of three fishermen from Massachusetts. This incident was also at Bosebuck Mountain Camps. One of the three gents was VERY new to fly fishing in particular and the woods in general. I had them for three days and it took me all of the first day and most of the second to convince him that he was not going to be attacked and eaten by a Maine bear! Somehow he had gotten the idea that bears were everywhere and that he was in peril constantly. I kept reassuring him that there were very few recorded examples of a Maine bear attacking anyone.

After a day and a half he was considerably calmer but I still would catch him looking over his shoulder as he was wading the Magalloway River and casting his fly. By day three, he actually had begun to relax and enjoy himself, and I could begin to teach him things about the Maine woods, other than bear.

The last afternoon, we had driven out to Route 16 to fish what we called the lower section of the Magalloway River. They were heading home when we left the water that afternoon, so they had followed me out and parked their vehicle near mine on Route 16. When we came to the place where we would step out of the river, hustle up over the riverbank and go our separate ways, we reeled up the fly rods and started to climb the bank into the paved road.

As it happened, when we cleared the edge of the bank, you had to step over an old log that was in the path. I was in the lead and was more intent on them than where I was stepping and as my bear-phobic customer stepped over the log, he looked down and said, "What the ___ is that?" He had stepped into a pile of fresh bear droppings that you couldn't have covered with a dinner plate. When I told him what it was, he let out a scream, dropped his fly rod, which he had fortunately put in its case, and ran at full speed up the road to where his truck was parked, certainly over a hundred yards, yelling every step of the way.

When he got to his truck, he fumbled around and got the keys out of his wader pocket, unlocked the vehicle, jumped inside and locked the doors. If his companions and I had been lying in the middle of the road, with a pulp truck coming at full bore, we couldn't have saved ourselves and would have been run over. We laughed until our sides ached and tears ran down our cheeks. Maybe I should have told him that it was moose doo-doo. In what was no surprise to me, he never returned.

Working on the log drives of yesteryear was brutally tough and extremely dangerous work. Those days were long before the advent of Gore-Tex and Thinsulate for warmth. This is to say nothing of safety regulations and equipment later designed to protect the river men.

My grandfather's lumbering business saw the men living in the woods all winter, getting the logs and pulp to the banks of the Dead River in western Maine for the spring drive down the Dead. One of my gramp's brothers was killed one spring on the drive. There was a log jam in the river, and he was one of the crew who were tasked with the job of dislodging it. Dislodging a jam was sometimes done with dynamite. In my great-uncle's case the jam suddenly let go and he was in the wrong place. They managed to get him out of the water, but he'd been crushed by the logs and he died as they got him back to the lumber camp.

Gramp was a lumberman and operated logging camps in the Flagstaff area for many years. In many ways, life for these men was fairly primitive. This absolutely was not a vocation for the faint-hearted. The crews were housed in long, narrow, low-roofed camps made of spruce logs. Naturally, the camps were heated by wood with at least one and sometimes two big wood stoves, sometimes called ram-down stoves. Monitor was a big name in the heater stoves used in these camps. Sleeping arrangements were a long bunk on each side that ran the entire length of the camp. These beds featured straw-filled mattresses and the camps always smelled a little "pungent" with the odor of sweat, and socks and union suits hanging on the drying lines every night. The long bunks were usually covered by one long, continuous blanket that was made from felt or wool. This blanket covered all the men on one side of the camp. My mother, who grew up in and around these camps, told me that in the middle of the night, when somebody wanted to turn over, he would yell at the top of his lungs, "Turn!", and everybody would roll over.

Hygiene and cleanliness were often conspicuous by their absence and by mid-winter virtually everyone was "lousy" (bed lice).

Short of anything else, these log drivers and woods workers were incredibly tough and durable. Injuries were frequent and often treated with back woods medicine. These men worked and survived under the most difficult conditions. There were no days off due to rain or snow. Days were long and began with a before-daylight breakfast and then it was off to the woods.

Somewhere around mid-day the cook and his cookee (kitchen helper) would show up with a horse-drawn sled or wagon loaded with the lunches. Hot tea, beans (beans were literally a staple of every meal), sandwiches, biscuits, and desserts rounded out the lunch menu. I have my grandfather's lunch pail. It is shaped like a fat submarine, with a removable top that has a round lid. The removable top was hollow and hot coffee or tea more likely was in the top. This was done in part so that in the winter, the lunches wouldn't freeze. The loggers ingested incredible amount of sweets and sugar which helped to provide the extreme, all-day energy that this work demanded.

One summer many years ago I worked for what was Scott Paper as a skidder operator. We worked that summer in an area called Middlesex Grant, on the west side of Moosehead Lake. Skidders are a very large sort of tractor with a winch and cables to haul logs, mounted on the back and a big blade in the front. My job was to bring the logs from where they were cut down to the wood yard, where they'd be piled in preparation for being loaded on the big trucks that would transport them to the mills.

Huge machines called harvesters were used for much of the wood to be cut, but there were also always crews of chain-saw cutters, all of whom were from Quebec. The boys from across the Canadian/U.S. border were mostly great guys and they were terrific loggers who cut enormous amounts of wood.

I was amazed watching the Canadians when we were eating breakfast in the camp dining room. The amounts of pure sugar they ingested were incredible. We all ate from steel cafeteria-type trays. The Canadians would pile their trays completely full of baked beans and bread. They'd literally cover the beans with a mound of sugar and grab a handful of cookies to stuff in their pockets. I was friendly with several of these Canadians and I asked once why they ate so much sugar and other sweets. It was explained to me that this was where their amazing amount of stamina came from. I've often wondered what if any later-in life results they had from eating so much sugar.

The summer that I spent working in the woods operating the skidder was one of the most enjoyable things that I've ever done. It made me feel as though I was, for a short time, part of something that played such a huge role in Maine's history.

That summer I got to know a couple of the old-timers who had been around the game for fifty or so years. They told me many stories of the old days in the woods. Many of these tales told of how, when the drives were over for the spring, they'd draw several months' pay. They'd head for Greenville or better yet, Bangor, for their annual "spree."

These down times were largely consumed with spending their winter wages. They went through money, liquor, and the company of ladies of questionable virtue very quickly. The sole purpose of these shady ladies was to separate these men from their wages in short order. Following these sprees, which usually concluded when they ran out of money, they'd return to the woods to start all over again.

Broke, rum-sick and ready to go back to work, they returned to the woods and the only life they knew. I asked one of the old-timers who shared many of these stories with me why they didn't try and save a little money. He made his point by saying, "By God boy, the times that we had!"

Maine's log drives on the rivers and lakes ended about fifty years ago. The end of the river drives brought the end of an era here in Maine that will never be seen again. Fortunately, many books and stories have been written about these days and the men that plied their trade on the rivers and in the woods. But, it is still sad to me to think that this is yet another way of life here in Maine that is gone forever. I am pleased and proud that I shared that life, even if only for a short time.

My dad's place in my life was relatively short-lived. Ma and Dad went their separate ways when I was four. I never really, truly got to know Dad until I was in the Navy and was stationed in Brunswick, Maine, a short ride from Dad's house and garage where we had lived until the divorce.

Dad was a hunter and a fisherman who supported his outdoor activities by being a very good auto mechanic. That all too short period of my life that he and I spent getting to know each other has always been very precious to me. I was very fortunate to be able to hear stories of his hunting and fishing adventures (and misadventures), many of which were in the company of Bob Wagg.

My favorite story about my dad centered on a trip that Dad, Bob, and two of their hunting cronies made to Aroostook County, ostensibly to hunt deer in October. This hunt was in the days when the deer season was open for at least the latter part of October. Dad had somehow made the acquaintance of an old fellow who was a guide and who'd taken a liking to Dad and referred to him as "Sonny." The old chap was kind of an itinerant sort, making ends meet by guiding, old-fashioned horse trading, and hunting his winter supply of meat each fall.

Dad and the boys were at the old geezer's camp and had decided to take the afternoon off from hunting because either the wind was blowing or it wasn't. The ensuing afternoon was occupied with poker, cribbage, copious amounts of spirits and regaling each other with stories of superior marksmanship.

Dad's weapon of choice in those days was a Model 740 Remington, chambered in .280 caliber. He was a hell of a shot with any kind of weapon and liked nothing better than showing off his ability with the .280. He explained how the gang had hung out at the camp on this particular day and that he had gone to some lengths to crow about how well he could shoot. The old guy hadn't had much to say until suddenly he stood up, reached into a corner and picked up an old, beat-up Winchester .38-55. The gun was so old that it had the hexagonal barrels and a magazine that would hold a dozen or so rounds of ammo. He grabbed the rifle, one round of ammunition and an empty liquor bottle. I am confident that there was no shortage of those. As he walked out the door, he said, "C'mon, Sonny!" and marched out to the area where his garden was located.

It was about eighty feet from one side of the garden to the other. It was surrounded by snow fence, although it's interesting to note that on the far side of the garden which abutted the woods there was a small gap in the fence not coincidently just wide enough for a deer to walk through.

Geezer walked to the far side of the garden and placed the liquor bottle on the top of a fence post, with the open end of the bottle facing the front side of the garden. Coming back across the garden where Dad and the others stood, he dropped the round into the gun, levered the round into the breach, and threw the gun up to his shoulder. Then with a split second of aiming, fired and blew the bottom out of the bottle without touching the neck. He turned to my father and said, "When you get so's you can shoot like that, Sonny, you come see me." This amazing display of shooting prowess, as Dad phrased it, pretty much ended all conversations about shooting.

Before he died, Dad told me about the last time that he shot a deer with the .280. He described looking up one morning and there, in the field across the road from his garage, stood two deer. When I asked if he was successful, his reply was to say that it didn't make much sense to go to all that effort for just one deer, so "I lifted both of 'em!"

I've always been thankful for the relatively short time that I could enjoy having my dad in my life. He was a hell of an outdoorsman, and at one time was thought of as one of the best auto mechanics in coastal Maine. Dad enjoyed life until the end and I suspect that at least part of my sense of humor and appreciation for a good story came from him. I still have his .280. Thanks, Dad.

Camps I Have Known

Over most of the last 70 years, I have had the distinct privilege of spending much of my life in cabins in a variety of places on two continents. Camps, especially those beautiful, old, sometimes pretty dilapidated structures built from logs native to the area, are my favorites. The stick-built camps are wonderful and special in their own right, but the log buildings have a very unique character.

My first camp experience was in a camp that was on the road that took you to the top of Eustis Ridge, looking down on Flagstaff Lake. This camp belonged to my grandfather who was a native of Flagstaff village. During those years when the tycoon JP Morgan owned Spring Lake Camps, near Flagstaff, Gramp and Grammie were the managers of those camps. My mother and aunt were food servers, and Gramp and JP were good friends. At some point, Morgan gave Gramp a one-room camp that was no longer being used.

Gramp had it moved from Spring Lake to a spot beside the church near Cathedral Pines. It didn't sit there for very long before Gramp had it moved again, this time to a lot that was about halfway up the Eustis Ridge Road. At one time, most of the camps on that road belonged to relatives of mine.

I can recall going to camp with Gramp to fish and hunt for partridge. Gramp was a very stout man and was supposed to be on a strict diet. Since Ma and I lived in Skowhegan with him, my mother did her best to watch his eating habits. However, when Gramp and I went to camp, a highlight of those trips would find us sneaking off to a brook someplace where we could catch a mess of brook trout.

The traditional Maine method of cooking trout is to render salt pork in an iron skillet, roll the trout in cornmeal and fry them in the grease. The salt pork cooked with the trout is delicious, and given the high level of salt, was certainly not on Gramp's diet. But, after all, we were at camp and none of that mattered. He and I would talk about not saying anything to Ma if she asked if he'd had too much pork. I've always been sure that she knew the truth anyway. The camp eventually became mine when Gramp passed.

The first time that I stayed in an honest to gosh log camp was when Uncle Ken took me, as a freshman in high school, to King & Bartlett camps, north of Eustis. K & B, as the locals called them, was owned at the time by a man named Deb Sylvester. The camps sat on the shore of King & Bartlett Lake, and there were numerous ponds within the area that offered excellent trout fishing. The original buildings were all hand-crafted log buildings that were built in the late 1800s. These were superbly made camps, heated with wood stoves and they were simply lovely.

One of my memories of these trips was that the beds all had the old, original feather mattresses. You could climb into one of those mattresses and just sink into a luxurious slumber, then wake up in the morning and look out on the lake and see the trout rising. To this day, I can remember how soft and comfortable those mattresses were. What a gift Uncle Bill gave me!

There was always an abundance of wildlife around the camps. Garbage and kitchen scraps were placed in 55-gallon drums which were on a fairly large utility trailer kept out behind the main lodge. The intent was that, as necessary, one of the staff would haul all the garbage, etc., off to a dump area located a long distance away from the camps. Each evening and at daylight, part of the entertainment was to watch the bears come to the garbage trailer and rummage in the barrels for food scraps. The last that I knew there were never any encounters between guests and bears. But when the bears visited, there was always someone from the camps there to supervise and be sure that the guests took their pictures from a respectful distance.

Lila and I launched Fins and Furs Adventures in January of 1987. Soon after, we were presented with an opportunity to market caribou hunts for an outfitter in the Delay River area of Quebec called Lac Luco Outfitters. I went up to the camps the first fall to guide for a month, the idea being to familiarize myself with things in order to better market them. Our camps were not classic log cabins. We stayed in tent camps, with wood stoves for heat, no running water and outhouses. When bath time came, we heated water in large metal buckets on the wood stove, peeled into our birthday suits and stood in the washtub that served as our bathtub. Hardly the ambiance of a snug log cabin!

There are a number of features and experiences that seem to be present in all of those beautiful old log buildings. Propane lights and cook stove, bunks attached to the walls, big wood stoves with tin stovepipes exiting through a wall or the roof and, naturally, a resident population of mice. You can lie in bed at night, after a great day afield, listening to the mice lull you to sleep as they scurry around in a cupboard or the sink cabinet. One of their habits that is harmless but takes some getting used to is feeling them race across your feet during the night.

We used to deer hunt with a good friend who had a camp in a fairly remote area. For reasons known only to him, he spent the fall waging a constant battle with the mice for supremacy of the camp. He'd have six or eight mouse traps set at any time, and we were woken nightly by the snap of mousetraps going off. Every time that he'd hear a trap go off, he'd laugh and say, "I got that little son of a bitch!"

There is a camp on Ellis Pond, in the area near the West Forks, where our camp is located. This camp is in a very sad state of collapse and every time we fish Ellis we put the canoes in right beside this old camp. This camp is quite special to me because it once belonged to a very well-known outdoor writer. Gene Letourneau was a sports writer for the Gannet Corporation, who used to publish the Morning Sentinel that we read to this day. Gene wrote a column called "Sportsmen Say," and was a wonderful man who I am proud to say was a good friend of mine.

Many years ago, the boys from the Wardens Worry Social Club went to Ellis for the evening trout hatch. Rather than go directly out on the water, I decided to poke around Gene's camp. Gene had been gone for many years by this time, and the camp had collapsed. I looked around the ruins of the camp and in a cardboard box found a set of dishes that had been used in Gene's camp. Most of them were broken, but I managed to find a plate, saucer, and cup that were intact. I brought them back to our camp that evening, washed them up and carefully put them in a secure place.

We still have them to this day and every now and then I'll use Gene's coffee cup, either for my morning coffee or my afternoon cup of insect repellant. In either case, I am positive that Gene, knowing him as I did, would have smiled in approval. Thanks, Gene!

In our travels over the years in not only Maine, but Newfoundland, New Brunswick, Quebec and Labrador, I've seen hundreds of these beautiful old log camps being left unattended and going to seed. I've seen roofs falling in, doors barely hanging on by one hinge, and the building simply falling apart due to lack of care. It has always saddened me to see these beautiful old camps in this state. Imagine, if the walls could talk, think of the stories that they could tell.

I love to duck hunt, although I do less of it now as seriously as I used to. We still have duck guns, decoys, canoes, boat and motor, etc. Unfortunately, time seems to get in the way of duck hunting and consequently, we have to decide between chasing the ducks and getting our 80-pound elephant, disguised as a Labrador Retriever, Riffle, into the upland covers. Riffle has matured into a great hunting dog. He has a fantastic nose, has established his range to within decent shooting distance and will sooner or later pick up every bird that we shoot and put it in my hand. It doesn't hurt that he is very bright and is an inherently funny dog.

We have an old friend who unfortunately is past his duck hunting days now, but someone that we spent a great deal of time with in the woods for one reason or another. He shared a story once with us that is too good not to relate. It seems that our friend and a couple of other hunters went duck hunting on Great Moose Pond in Harmony. Moose Pond is a fairly large lake with coves and marshes that provide excellent waterfowl habitat. One of these coves is called Pickerel Cove, much of which is ideal duck country. At the mouth of Pickerel Cove there is a point with lots of large rocks above the waterline that provide great chances for hunters to tuck in behind where you can ambush the ducks as they fly into the cove to feed.

One of my friend's companions (we'll call him Bill) was notoriously frugal (read stingy) about most things, including his firearms. His duck gun of choice was a Stevens twelve-gauge, single-barrel shotgun, that I used to tease him about by saying that it was certainly of Civil War vintage. The gun was ancient, rusty and worst case would occasionally misfire, usually when most needed. The group decided that since Bill had only a single-shot gun, while the others were using pump guns, that Bill would tuck in behind some of the rocks on the point where he could shoot as the ducks came soaring into the cove. The theory was that Bill could only fire one shot and once he'd done that any surviving ducks would fly to the back of the cove where the rest of the hunters were waiting in a real duck blind that they'd built.

The group was positioned in their respective places well before daylight, and the wait began. Soon after the onset of legal light, from across the lake came a huge flight of Canada geese, numbering in the hundreds. As the geese reached the point where Bill waited, instead of flying past him the entire flight dropped into the water directly in front of where Bill was concealed behind the rocks.

As his companions watched, Bill rose up from behind the rocks, shouldered his weapon and apparently pulled the trigger. Dead silence. Bill's worn-out shotgun had once again failed to fire. They watched as Bill went back down behind the rocks, opened the breech, took out the round that had failed to fire and inserted a second round. The entire process was repeated. Bill rose up, pulled the trigger and the gun failed to discharge. Back behind the rocks, they watched as Bill changed rounds yet again, and rose up from behind the rocks with round number three in the chamber. For the third time, Bill's gun refused to fire. He lowered the gun and removed the round. However, this time, instead of reloading the gun, Bill stood up, grabbed the shotgun by the front end of the barrel, and threw it like a boomerang out in the midst of the geese and yelled at the top of his lungs, "Here she comes, boys!"

In the next instant, the entire flock of geese immediately went into sheer panic. The air was full of feathers and geese frantically trying to get off the water and the hell out of there! Geese were flying in every direction, including towards the back of the cove where the other hunters waited.

When my friend related this story to me, I couldn't stop laughing, with tears running down my cheeks. When I could stop laughing long enough, I asked my friend if they shot any of the geese as they flew out over the back of the cove. His reply was that they were lying on the grass in the blind in convulsive laughter, and couldn't have picked up their guns if their lives had depended on it.

Bill never made any effort to retrieve his shotgun. To the best of my knowledge, it still lies in a couple of feet of water, by the point on Pickerel Cove. Truth to tell, it probably would work as well today as it did when Bill had it. For the record, Bill's companions chipped in and bought him another single-barrel twelve-gauge.

My old friend Chet, Lila, and I hunted together for years, largely ducks and upland birds. During the entire fiasco, we decided that Lila and I needed a duck dog to go along with our upland dogs, the Blackfield Pointers. A retired game warden that was a relative of our friend bred his female Lab to one of our friend's stud dogs. Taking a pup, Lila and I were in the duck dog business. Our Lab, whose name was Deke (short for "decoy," pretty catchy, huh?) was a full brother to a male that Chet kept.

As the dogs made their way through their first year, their training continued and eventually came to the point in their development when we needed live birds to train with and to develop their water retrieval skills. Keep in mind that each of these Labs now weighed somewhere around 80 pounds. This would become much more important later.

There was a beautiful bog, shaped like a figure eight, a couple of miles from Chet's house. We managed to get our hands on an all white domestic duck who reluctantly volunteered to be the subject of this training exercise. We took both dogs, a canoe and the duck to the bog and worked out a very elaborate plan to replicate actual hunting conditions. The plan was for us to put the dog, duck and us in a canoe, paddle out to a wooded point in the bog where I was to go ashore, and hide in the trees. Then we'd put the duck, whose wings were taped so that he couldn't fly, on the water. When Chet was at the canoe launch with his dog, I was to blow on the duck call and fire a shot, all in full view of Chet's Lab. Chet was going to line the dog up, give him a mark to determine the direction that he was supposed to swim in and release him.

This really was a great plan except for a few minor details. First, nobody told the dog or the duck what was expected. We neared the point and Chet threw the shackled duck into the water. Since we weren't bright enough to hold the dog, as soon as Chet tossed the duck into the water, Chet's dog, whose name was Amos, jumped up and left the canoe, all 80 pounds of him, by pushing off the gunwale of the canoe with his hind legs.

When a significant amount of weight is suddenly placed on the gunwale of a canoe, several things happen, none of them good! First the canoe immediately inverts itself in the water and becomes upside down. This alone causes the canoe to become, briefly we hope, submerged. Getting ourselves out of this predicament was no small job.

Fortunately, the water was shallow enough so that we could stand up, but we were not a pretty pair. Beyond being soaking wet we were covered in mud and bog weeds, many of which were sticking to our clothes. We both had beards and our beards collected various water plants so that we both bore a resemblance to a swamp creature. We wallowed our way back to the canoe launch, accompanied by Amos, who thought this entire exercise was terrific—Dad and Uncle Carroll went swimming with me!

All of this matter was further compounded by the fact that we didn't want our wives to know about this little escapade. Chet's grandfather was a wonderful eighty-something old gent whom Lila and I loved dearly. One of his great pleasures in life was to catch Chet and me in one of our fiascos and immediately inform our wives.

To get back to Chet's house, we had to drive directly past the trailer that Grandfather lived in. As we passed his trailer, we slid down in the truck seats so that hopefully he wouldn't see us. All was well as we passed his place and pulled into Chet's driveway. We stepped out of the truck, covered in mud, dripping water with various plants hanging off us. As we stepped out, around the corner of the barn comes Grandfather. Grandfather had eyes as blue as flint and as he came up the driveway towards us, he never so much as looked at us. However, as he walked past us, he looked at us from the corner of his eye and said, "I'd of thought if you boys were goin' swimmin' you'd have found someplace with a sandy bottom." With that said, he moseyed up the driveway and on to his house.

It goes without saying that the wives were waiting for us when we got to the dog kennels.

I wouldn't go so far as to say that I've guided customers from Hell, but I have had two or three that were half-way.

Let me be very clear; speaking for Lila and me, 95% of the people with whom we have come into contact have been wonderful. They have been people that we guided, or people that we arranged hunting or fishing trips for with one of the outfitters that we've represented over the last 34 years. Maybe they were among the several thousand people who participated in our Maine Guide's training programs, but regardless, nearly all of them were terrific people.

Truth to tell, though, there have been a few trying moments. Sometimes difficult moments occur because somebody just doesn't listen. More likely, it's because they think that they know more than you do about the subject at hand. During the Bosebuck years one May, I guided a gal from Massachusetts and her husband for a couple days of ice-out fly fishing. They were nice people; the husband was an experienced fly fisherman, the wife was not. She had been to three days of LL Bean's fly fishing school. Usually, this would have been fine, but the lady believed EVERY single word that the LLB instructor had said to her and she could remember them verbatim. Every time that I'd make a suggestion to help her casting, her reply would be, "Well, the man at LL Bean said," and on and on. I tried to make her understand that casting conditions in casting school were one thing but that casting under field conditions were an entirely different kettle of fish.

We went through the morning and by lunch she had really tested my patience. Over sandwiches and hot tea, I tried to explain that she couldn't always use textbook tactics as she had been taught, rather she needed to adapt to conditions around her.

There is a run of water above the #10 bridge on the Parmachenee Road, at the head of Aziscohos Lake, that we called back then Cedar Run Pool. This pool was a 200' run of slick water with variances in water depth and a rocky bottom that held many lies, some of which were tough to spot. The lady was at the head of the pool with me and I wanted to help her wade twenty or thirty feet out into the pool so that she could reach the far side of it with a cast. When you step off the bank into this pool, quite near the top of the run, you can safely take two steps but then there is a drop or a trough that is a foot deeper than the water on either side of it. She was a very inexperienced wader and didn't have the sense to go slowly.

As I held her arm to help her into the run, her husband yelled for me because he had hooked a beautiful salmon and needed my help to land it. I told her specifically to stay put and I'd be back in a moment. I went downstream, netted her husband's salmon. When I looked up stream to where she had been, there she was, teetering her way out into the water, specifically what I had told her not to do. I yelled for her to stop but she ignored me. She took two steps and dropped right into the deeper spot, clean out of sight for a moment.

The water temperature was 56°F that day. As the current carried her downriver towards me, I just waited and when she floated by me I grabbed the collar of her shiny new fly-fishing vest and stood her up. When I had her on her feet and she was done spurting water out of her mouth, she said a VERY bad word. Fortunately it was not directed at me but more at the temperature of the water. Odd as it was, her dip in the Magalloway seemed to get her attention; for the rest of the day her ability to listen to me improved significantly and she actually caught some fish.

We once had a call from a man who lived in the Portland area. He was an executive with one of Maine's major grocery store chains. His role with this corporation was working with suppliers and vendors, procuring food and other products. His was a very lofty position that required much travel nationally. He contacted us, asking about three days of upland bird hunting over our pointing dogs for himself and three of his more prominent suppliers.

We agreed on dates and rates and I was to pick the area where we hunted.

I chose to hunt them in the areas between the West Forks and Jackman, in part because Lila and I are part owners in a camp there, and next, because this is a vast area of big woods that usually provides excellent shooting for grouse and woodcock. The other reason behind my choice was an inn located in The Forks called The Inn by The River. This is a beautiful facility providing excellent lodging, meals and amenities, all overlooking the Kennebec River. We have used this as lodging for our customers many times over the years.

All four of these men were simply great guys. They were gentlemen, excellent hunters, who were easy to be around and also were obviously successful financially. We had a terrific time together for three days. At the end of each day, they invited me to join them at the Inn for a cocktail to celebrate another successful day.

It's worth mentioning that the shotguns that these men carried were emphatically not Sears and Roebuck guns. All four of them carried very expensive shotguns and they all could shoot well. Of great importance to me as their guide was that they were safe hunters and I never once in three days had to make any comments about gun safety. As will be seen later, this is not always the case. The gentleman who'd organized the hunt drove a Chevrolet Suburban with all the bells and whistles. The guns were always stored in expensive leather cases, custom designed for each particular gun.

When the last afternoon came to a halt and we returned to the inn, they each handed me a very generous cash gratuity. At the end of our afternoons we all enjoyed martinis made with one of my favorite vodkas, Grey Goose. As we parted, they gave me a large bottle of Grey Goose on top of my gratuities. Verbal commitments were offered for the following season and a repeat of this year's hunt. I enjoyed three of the most pleasant days that I had spent with any customers that entire year. Apparently, I also could look ahead to repeat business the next fall.

The winter passed and as spring began to roll around, I thought about sending a note to all our upland hunting customers suggesting that this would be a great time to reserve the fall hunting days with us. Imagine my surprise when one morning in April, as Lila and I sat down for our to-this-day morning ritual of newspaper and coffee, I read the news and nearly fell out of my chair.

The executive from the grocery chain had been indicted for fraud, theft and embezzlement. Wow! No wonder he drove a luxury vehicle and hunted with a shotgun worth several thousand dollars. He wound up with a prison sentence of several years and lost everything that he had, including his family. This reinforces the old saying about not judging a book by its cover.

I have had on at least two different occasions, with different parties, the unusual but very interesting experience of guiding men who were what is commonly referred to as "connected." By that term I refer to their association with a group that has long been considered to be a part of the crime underworld. On both of these occasions, the activity was upland bird hunting. I'm not sure what it is about this activity that seems to attract people with questionable vocations.

The first of these two groups were elevator service technicians from New York City. They had hundreds of mob stories, among them was the story that one of them told of his time as a youth in the city. His dad had relationships with "the boys," as he described them. He told several stories about when he was a teenager, and a man from "out of town" would come and stay at their house. His comment was that when the stranger showed up, somebody was going to get "whacked." The man would come, sure enough there would be a shooting and he'd leave until the next time.

One of the things that was astonishing to me was that they related this story and many others as though they were describing a hunting trip. I suppose that in a roundabout way, that's just what they were doing. One of the more chilling quotes that I heard during the five days that I was guiding them was that nobody needed to look under the New York Giants stadium for Jimmy Hoffa because he wasn't there, rather he was "feeding the fishes."

The other man that I guided owned office buildings and made absolutely no bones about at least some of his tenants. His comment was, "Sure, I rent to the Mafia, no big deal."

Moments like these and many others always were reminders of how secure our lives in Maine are. It is amazing to me that people actually lived like this on a day to day basis.

Usually, the most egregious moments for guides involve firearms. Most often these issues happen because the hunting customers are either inexperienced or just plain old careless. A party of two hunters that I guided last fall on a moose hunt was among the most careless that I have ever worked with.

On opening morning, as we drove to the hunting areas, I gave them my standard safety lecture and assumed that I had made myself very clear. Literally from the first step into the woods, it became a nightmare. Guns were pointed at my vehicle, at each other and at me. This quickly turned the hunt into repeated warnings and ultimately a confrontation that ended my participation in their hunt two days early. I came away from this hunt so frustrated that I made the decision that my career as a hunting guide is more than likely over.

I have had two incidents, one with another upland hunter and the other with a deer hunter and his son that nearly resulted in a loss of life. One of those lives nearly lost was mine and the other was a father, at the hands of his fifteen-year-old son. I won't detail either of these events because they are very uncomfortable memories and both have always been great reinforcement for my belief that as guides, regardless of the circumstance, we often are a deep breath or a trigger pull away from a life-threatening moment. Did I mention that we don't get paid enough to endure these kinds of risks?

Sometimes customers seem to be absolutely determined to get themselves in a mess, one way or the other. Over the years, we have marketed elk and mule deer hunts for two or three outfitters in Colorado and Montana. I took two gents from southern Maine to Colorado with me one November for an elk hunt. One of them was simply just a great guy to hunt with and the other was, shall we say, very, very difficult. He refused to listen to anyone, including me and the outfitter, about any given topic. His stock answer was, "Yeah, I know that."

One of the hazards with high-altitude hunts in the Western mountains is altitude sickness. This malady can be extremely dangerous and life threatening. It's also very easy to prevent by doing two simple things: eat plenty and drink LOTS of water.

I'd hunted in Montana a few years before this hunt, and after the second night, I was having headaches and difficulty sleeping. I mentioned it to the outfitter's wife and she asked how much water I was consuming during the day. My reply was that I was taking in about thirty ounces during the day. Her comment was, "Triple that." That evening I started pouring massive amounts of water into me, and from that point on, I was drinking ninety ounces of water daily, and slept like a baby all night long.

My difficult customer on the Colorado trip just wasn't going to buy into the water consumption method, mostly because he was stubborn. The day before our hunt started we'd gone into the mountains to the outfitter's tents camp, which was located at about eighty-five hundred feet. On day three, at the end of the day, smart-guy walked into the cook tent and announced that he was having trouble buttoning the buttons on his shirt. Loss of physical dexterity is one sign of the advance of altitude sickness. The outfitter told the hunter to pack up because his guide was going to take him off the mountain. He was taken off the mountain and didn't return. The rest of us who'd done what we were told, harvested elk. "What's his name" spent the remainder of the trip at the base lodge, with no refund and no further hunting.

I am quite convinced of two things: First, that most guides would agree with me that nearly all of our customers are simply terrific people who we would spend a month with if we could. Next, that while most of us have at one time or another had these frightening moments with customers, we love what we do. And as professionals we take great pains to see that these scary moments are as infrequent as possible. The good news is that if these questionable customers call again, we can say, "Gee whiz, I am booked solid."

Over the last thirty-three and more years that Lila and I have owned and operated Fins and Furs Adventures, we have both served the Maine Department of Inland Fisheries & Wildlife (IF&W) in several capacities. Lila served as a member of IF&W's Advisory Council, representing Somerset and Piscataquis Counties. I served for twelve years as a member of the Maine Guide's Advisory Board, acting as one of the oral examiners. We have both worked on several projects with IF&W over the years, developing a high level of respect for the professionals of the Maine Warden Service.

During this long association with IF&W we have had the opportunities to share relationships with any given number of game wardens. As a result, we have had the privilege of hearing many, many stories of searches for lost people, chasing poachers through the woods in the dark and other accounts of often extremely funny, and some not so funny, incidents.

One of our favorite wardens was a fellow who lived in Bingham named Wallace Barron. Wally served as a warden for nearly twenty-five years. He and his wife Crystal owned a camp near Lac Megantic in Quebec, which is barely over the border from Maine. Wally and I were sitting in a duck blind there one bluebird day. It was such a nice, sunny day that the only birds flying were sea gulls. Wally started to ramble on with stories about some of the escapades that he'd experienced in his years as a warden. One of my favorites to this day involves Wally's years of service in eastern Maine.

It seems there was an older gentleman that Wally had been after for several years. He told me that once in a great while, he could nab him with a "short" (too small to be legal) trout, or maybe a grouse or two over the legal limit. But in Wally's words,

"I could never catch him doing something that I could charge him with and really put him away for a while."

Finally, one October, Wally received a tip from an informant that the old fellow had poached a moose and was intending to sell the meat to anyone who had the cash. The old violator lived in a log camp that he'd built himself. There also was a woodshed and a large garden plot behind the camp. Oddly enough, the guy had planted his garden mostly to turnips and broccoli, both of which deer love to eat. Get the idea? The tip was that the old poacher had moose meat in his camp and in the woodshed.

Wally and his fellow officers planned their visit very carefully. They knew that they would have to depend on the element of total surprise if they were going to be able to nab him this time after so many fruitless tries. Wally went to a local judge, explained the circumstances and obtained a search warrant. The day of the raid, Wally and his fellow wardens made a careful and detailed plan. They would arrive in two pickups, charging into the yard of the camp. Two of the wardens would rush into the woodshed and Wally and his partner would charge into the camp, all hopefully before the suspect had time to hide anything.

The fateful hour came and two pickups loaded with game wardens came roaring into the camp yard. The two wardens who were assigned the wood shed ran into the woodshed and sure enough, there were four freshly-skinned quarters of moose meat hanging in the shed. Wally and his partner burst through the door of the camp yelling loudly, "Game wardens, don't move!"

Sure enough, they found the sink full of moose liver and heart, as they'd been told. They also found the old poacher, sitting in his rocking chair, stone dead! Apparently, all the exertion of handling the moose had caused the old fellow to have a massive cardiac event, and he'd died right there in his chair. As Wally told this story, he actually smiled and when he'd finished the tale he said, "That old S.O.B. foiled us right to the very end."

On another occasion with Wally in a duck blind, he related a story about his pursuit of a fellow who was a dedicated, life-long poacher. This particular miscreant took great pleasure in eluding wardens by saying, "Them wardens ain't smart enough to catch me poachin'." In the eyes of the wardens, he was the worst kind of poacher because he wasn't poaching deer to feed his family. He killed deer illegally for the sole purpose of selling the meat for his own profit.

This poacher eluded the warden service for many years until finally, on a snowy Thanksgiving morning, Wally received a tip that the poacher had shot a couple of dozen deer over the previous week or so. The tipster also shared the news that those deer had all been hidden in a tractor trailer load of Christmas trees that was headed for Massachusetts the next morning. Wally got the description of the truck and the logo on the truck doors.

When the truck approached the toll gate on the Maine Turnpike on the south end, the wardens were waiting and the truck was pulled over and searched. Upon searching the load of trees, there they were—more than two dozen deer that were heading for market in Massachusetts. The old poacher very shortly became the guest of Somerset County for a year.

The role of Maine game wardens has evolved significantly over time. Sometimes, by necessity, wardens are involved in domestic disputes and many other non-wildlife cases that detract from their usual duties. Gary Anderson was the safety officer and search & rescue coordinator for IF&W for many years. He shared two typical stories of his career.

The first involved a call from an anxious wife in Fairfield whose husband had left early that November morning, ostensibly for a day of deer hunting. When he failed to return in a reasonable amount of time that evening, she placed a call to the Warden Service and reported him as a lost person who was several hours late. Once Gary was notified a team of wardens and other searchers was assembled. Information was provided by the hunter's wife, indicating that her husband had planned to hunt in the Unity area, which he had done before.

Considerable time and effort was put into this search but no sign of the hunter was found. The search was further complicated by the fact that his vehicle was not located in the area where his

wife indicated that he would be. As the evening wore on, interviews with other hunters and friends began to indicate that perhaps all was not what it appeared to be. At or around 2:00 a.m.
the next morning, the lost hunter was located in Winslow at the
apartment of a young lady who was obviously an "acquaintance"
of his. Gary said that he never learned the ultimate result of the
discovery and what ensued after the news was conveyed to his
wife. Chances are that there *were* consequences.

The other story that Gary shared struck close to home with
Lila and me because it happened in the area of Bosebuck Camps.
Directly across Aziscohos Lake from Bosebuck Camps lies Green
Top Mountain. There is a road that you can see from the sporting
camps that goes directly east right up over Green Top and on to
Coburn Gore. Gary related the story of getting a call from a group
of upland bird hunters one October. They reported about 9:00
p.m. that one of the members of their group had not returned that
afternoon.

A team was assembled and after interviews with members of
the group the search began. According to the group, the lost
hunter had no bird dogs with him and had just planned to walk
several old roads. The search continued through the night per
usual. Signal shots were fired by the game wardens all night long,
but no responses were ever heard.

At approximately 9:00 a.m. the next morning one of the wardens was in his truck returning to the command post. As he
rounded a corner in the Green Top Road, there was a hunter who
fit the description of the lost person walking along the gravel road.
The warden stopped and picked up the man and returned with
him to the trailer that was serving as the command post.

As Gary was interviewing the hunter in an effort to discover
the details of the man's night, the hunter asked Gary if he could
say something. Gary of course said that any information that
could be provided might prove useful to the department in future
searches in that area. The hunter, who had been in the woods all
night long while searchers were firing gunshots in an effort to

locate him, looked at Gary and said, "Mr. Anderson, you've got a hell of a night hunting problem here."

This story made the rounds of IF&W for quite some time.

As much as I love to fish those small, remote trout ponds, my heart truthfully lies in the moving water. I've never been exactly sure why I am so captured by rivers. Perhaps it's the aesthetics of rivers, the constantly changing surface, and the often gentle, subtle sounds that rivers create as they make their way to the sea. Maybe it's how suddenly, often just a step around a bend in the river, that the complexion of things changes, from soft and gentle to raging and loud. When I return to a river that I haven't fished for a while, it's like seeing an old friend whom I really care about but haven't been with for a long time.

My favorite part of the day on a river is at first light of day. There is something about watching, waiting for the river to wake up, that can make me feel very insignificant. I love to just sit there and watch as the river comes to life. I can watch the birds, see the first few fish that begin their day by dimpling the surface of the water. For a little while, I can forget about the crazy world that is out there. Eventually, it dawns on me that I came to fish and I begin to come to life.

Lila and I have fished many, many rivers on two continents. Somehow, much of the time, I have managed to be on the wrong side of the river. I learned at a young age that there will always be two or three set-in-stone facts about fishing rivers. One of them is that the biggest fish in the river will always be several feet farther than I can reach with a cast. Another is that there will nearly always be an alder or a beautiful birch that inhibits my fly cast. More commonly, I realized that despite changing sides of the river sometimes more than once, invariably I am on the wrong side of the river. That long, deep run that looks incredibly trout-ish is more than a long cast away. I cross the river to take advantage of a run of water that will allow me to present my fly in a natural drift that any self-respecting trout couldn't possibly refuse. Once I've crossed, I realize that there is an eddy line below a rock that I couldn't see and I have no way to get a natural drift.

The next thing that the passing of time has gifted me with is that my feet don't seem to always go where I think they are going. This has resulted in a few monumental but unscheduled dips into the river. Years ago, Lila and I were on one of our many trips to Quebec's Broadback River. I slipped off a rock and other than the top two feet of my fly rod, went completely out of sight into the Broadback. This was made even more humiliating by the fact that this happened in full view of Lila. As if that wasn't' enough, I had just lit my last Cuban Cohiba cigar! It took two days of drying on the wood stove in our camp until I could get it to light again.

There is a pool on what is probably my favorite river, the Kennebec, called Stand-Up Rips. I am sure that this pool was named by one of those long-forgotten river drivers who used to work the river every spring. Stand-Up is a long, slick pool that flows out of a big curve in the river, just below where Moxie Stream enters the Kennebec.

I love this pool, I've guided many of our fly-fishing customers to it and it rarely disappoints me. The pool shoals up at the end and there is a ledge that makes out into the river. This ledge creates a beautiful run of water that is best fished with a streamer, my favorite being the Black Ghost. This particular fly pattern was created many years ago by a famous taxidermist and fly tier in Rangeley, Herb Welch. Stand-Up was one of the areas in the Kennebec where log jams frequently occurred. Downriver from Stand-Up lies another piece of water that is very dear to me. Many years ago, because of the abundance of cedar trees that hang out over the water on the west side of the pool, I named this pool The Cedars.

I started fishing this particular stretch of water nearly fifty years ago (it seems like there are an awful lot of places that I started fishing fifty or so years ago). I have spent literally hundreds upon hundreds of hours in this particular stretch of this beautiful river.

The Kennebec is only a couple of hundred feet wide in this area. Virtually this entire run of water is wadeable ("wadeable" is a word that fly fishermen made up long ago). It isn't so much a classically beautiful pool as it is just a long, smooth run of slick water. A feature of this piece of the river is that the far bank is in the shadows until mid-day, and the trout and salmon will lie in those shadowed areas.

The river above this spot kind of chuckles and giggles as it runs over the riffles and then into the slick area. There are a number of big rocks in this area that provide shelter, and great places for a lazy brook trout to lie in wait for a caddis fly to drift by. This becomes a long, smooth pool that is simply beautiful. It is a fairly quiet run, but I love to just be there and listen to the water talk to me. Usually, there will be fish rising the length of the pool but this pool can be hard to fish. There are only three or so feet of water in most of it and the water here is very clear, making it very easy to spook fish. When I fish The Cedars, I spend as much time just standing and watching as I do casting. Often, my morning is pleasantly interrupted by a flight of mergansers as they make their way up the river. If I am fortunate as I stand in the water one of the area's resident eagles will soar over my head, reminding me that Fang and Macklin are saying good morning.

I don't get to Stand-up or The Cedars as much anymore, it just always seems as though there is work around the camp that needs doing or I am on my way to an area pond for the evening hatch. I did promise Lila that she and I would share some of those early-morning hours soon. True to my word, a lovely May morning found us on the river.

I was fishing a slick just above what we call the ledges and Lila was below me. Each of us, on our very first cast, hooked and landed a salmon. We released the salmon and I made my way down to Lila until I was behind her on the ledges. She turned to speak to me, taking a step as she did, and her feet went out from under her and she suddenly disappeared in three feet of Kennebec River water. All that I could see was the tip section of her fly rod! She had some trouble getting her feet under her and as I made my way out to help her, she surfaced, sputtering and laughing. After she was on her feet, I mentioned that I would have given her a nine-point five for style points. I trust that you'll understand if I don't share her response.

How could I not find the means to spend a few hours where I can listen to the water talk to me, be entertained by its silence, and leave me with my memories of friends and hours lost? Every time that I am fortunate to spend a few hours on this part of the river, I am always moved as I recall the endless memories I have on this river and how blessed I am to have shared those times with my dearest friends.

During the thirty-five years we have owned and operated Fins and Furs Adventures, we have enjoyed (endured on occasion) many outfitters whose business we represented and provided customers for.

In this span of time, there have been many, many memorable moments. In another chapter, I detailed several of our escapades with Richard Demers, who owned the Broadback River Fishing Camps. When it came to protecting his resource, in this case, trophy brook trout, Richard was a genius. In other aspects of the outfitter business, Richard was a poster boy for how not to run a sporting camp. Fortunately, the positives far outweighed the negatives and we had a twelve-year run with Richard that was a great success and helped us begin our journey as hunting and fishing consultants.

At one point, we sold caribou hunts on Quebec's Ungava Peninsula for a company named Arctic Adventures, based in Montreal. The hunting manager was a delightful man named Denis LaPointe. Denis was a character with a great sense of humor and a world of experience in dealing with the general public. He was a retired detective for the Royal Canadian Mounted Police in Montreal. During his last few years as a detective Denis was an undercover agent who specialized in dealing with the drug trade that was coming from Southeast Asia.

When Denis shared this story with me, it sent chills down my spine. It seems that during one of his drug transactions while he was in Los Angeles, his cover was somehow compromised and the bad people realized what he was up to. As Denis related this story to me, the drug gang had him in a warehouse in LA. They had broken both his wrists and were about to cut off his hands when the cavalry burst through the door and saved him.

In part because of his experience in law enforcement, Denis had a very philosophical outlook on life that extended to his work as a hunting manager. During one of our conversations when we were trying to come to an agreement about a certain issue, he finally threw his hands up and said, "Carroll, if our businesses are gonna get in bed together, what difference does it make who takes their pants off first?" Denis and I never had a problem working together after that. Denis, rest in peace, mon ami.

In another chapter, we mention a man named Capt. Ed Bayer, for whom we marketed the fantastic fishing in the Florida Keys. In addition to being a man who had many talents, Ed loved playing practical jokes at every opportunity as much as I do. During his twenty-plus year career, Ed was an executive at the national level for Enterprise Car Rental, and worked directly with the owner. Following Ed's retirement to his home in Duck Key, Florida, Ed would host a group of his former Enterprise business associates in the Keys for an annual Mahi-Mahi (dolphin fish) tournament. Ed owned both a flats skiff and a thirty-foot offshore fishing boat.

As the annual tournament was coming closer, Ed would always set up some sort of practical gag to play on the boys. On this particular year, Ed found someone in the Keys who could get his hands on wrist watches that by all appearances were authentic Rolex luxury watches. Ed bought one of the Rolex "knock-offs" for the princely sum of fifty bucks and set the trap. During each of the first three days of trolling on the ocean, Ed made it a point to complain to anyone within earshot about how unhappy he was with his new "Rolex." He kept asking his fellow fishermen what time it was and then made a grand show of having to reset his watch.

Ed decided on the last day of the tournament to spring the trap. He was at the console of his boat, and asked what time it was. When one of the guys gave him the time, Ed apparently exploded, saying, "This son of a bitch hasn't worked right since I bought it, I paid five thousand bucks for this thing and I have had it." With this, Ed suddenly removed the watch from his wrist, held it by one end of the glitzy expansion band, smashed it on the console of his boat and threw it into the ocean.

According to Ed, there was absolute dead silence for about twenty seconds. Finally, Ed couldn't maintain his composure any longer and let everyone in on the joke. He described astonishment, then gales of laughter. If I could have ever gotten my hand on one of those watches, I would have pulled this one off in a heartbeat.

One of our most beloved clients was a man named Alain Tardiff. For more than twenty years, Alain owned and operated Leaf River Lodge in Quebec. The Leaf River runs from east to west, along the base of Quebec's famed Ungava Peninsula. Alain stood about five feet, seven inches and had a firecracker personality and was convinced that he could do anything that he set his mind toward.

Leaf River Lodge was located right on the banks of the Leaf River in the midst of a very remote area of Quebec known as Nunavik. The Leaf River is over a hundred miles inland from a large Inuit community called Kuujjuaq (pronounced koo'-juak). The Leaf River is a very large river and in some areas is impassable via water due to the extreme changes in elevation, which results in tremendous rapids. Consequently, the lodge was accessible only via float plane, typically twin-engine DeHaviland Otters.

For seventeen years, we sold caribou hunts and fishing adventures for Alain. We made at least one trip there in each of those years, bringing eight or ten customers with us. Every year was a great adventure. The process of reaching the lodge meant a flight via commercial aircraft from Montreal to a float plane base on Lake Caniapiscau, in the interior of Quebec, then a two-hour float plane ride over some of the most remote land anywhere in the world. The caribou hunts always were a terrific experience, and bear and wolves were often around following the caribou herds as they made their winter migration south. Fishing was simply amazing with brook and lake trout, and Atlantic salmon very plentiful.

One of the many stories that made Alain the legend that he was in our industry centered about his need to have a bulldozer at the camps. Alain was always working on some new way to make the camps more efficient and less dependent on the outside world. Once he decided that he had to have a bulldozer, the immediate question became how to get this machinery from Kuujjuaq to the camps. Anything that came to Kuujjuaq came either by air or by water as there was a seaport there. Once the dozer was in Kuujjuaq, the next problem became how to get it from the community to the camps.

Alain, being Alain, decided that he and his partner would build a small camp, which was on skids, and they would tow the camp, using the bulldozer, and sleeping in the heated camp all the way to the lodge. Readers must understand that this means that they would drive from the city to the camps, towing their only means of survival behind the dozer for well over a hundred miles. All this would be done during the severe Arctic winter. During the summer, diesel fuel for the machine was stashed at strategic points along the proposed route that they would follow and refuel as they traveled.

Departure day arrived with Alain driving the Case bulldozer towing the cabin, and his partner driving a snowmobile. Knowing Alain as I did, I can picture him driving the dozer, leaving safety and civilization behind, without a care in the world. He told me once that it never, for one moment, occurred to him that he wouldn't make it to the camps.

Needless to say, he arrived at the camps, after driving the Case machine for TWENTY-THREE days across the barren land that is Nunavik. Over the years after the bulldozer arrived at the Leaf, among other things he rebuilt his dock area on the waterfront (much to the displeasure of the Government of Quebec).

In my mind, Alain's most significant project, which he completed in the face of battling cancer for the last years of his life, was to complete his airstrip. In the midst of the Quebec wilderness, he built an 1800' gravel runway so that the Otter aircraft could reach the camps with wheeled aircraft versus float planes.

To this day, Alain's son, Louis, in a testament to his father's tenacity and determination continues to operate Leaf River Lodge.

In 2020, the cancer presented an obstacle that even Alain's stubborn determination couldn't overcome. Alain's family gave his ashes to the river that was home to him and where his spirit will remain forever.

During 2017, Lila and I made our last trip to the Leaf Camps, as the Government of Quebec had decided to close the caribou hunts due to concerns, correct or otherwise, about the Leaf River herd. We stayed with Alain at his private camp during our last visit. When it came time to board the Otter for the flight to Montreal and civilization, as Lila, Alain and I stood on the waterfront, waiting to board for the last time, Alain and I couldn't look at each other for fear of losing our emotions. Amidst tears we hugged each other and unwilling to say good-bye, said that we'd see each on the Leaf again someday. We lost Alain in the summer of 2020. I doubt that we'll visit the Leaf again, but a distinct part of both of us will always be there.

There are many things that the life I have led has given me that I really like. The many, many wonderful and influential people that I've come into contact with, moments in time that my pal Mother Nature has provided, and the list goes forward. So, I decided that in this chapter, I would try to talk about at least some of these things. I will warn the reader that my tastes sometimes range from eclectic to weird. I often find myself being attracted to things that no one else pays much attention to.

In no particular order of preference, I like various things for sometimes unusual reasons. For example, I like the little frogs that you find living in the pools created by skidder ruts in the twitch roads left by loggers. These little frogs, both amaze and amuse me. When I walk to my tree stand, there will be dozens of them, lined up on the edge of the pool, basking in the sunlight. When I am within ten or so feet, it's as if someone rings the alarm bell and they all disappear in a splash and a cloud of mud. What really fascinates me is that when the temperature reaches a certain number, these frogs get a message from somebody and they all apparently within a matter of moments simply disappear. I am confused that all of these frogs apparently get the message at the same time and they are gone. Beyond this, where can they go? When you are a three-inch frog, I should imagine that your options for winter survival are fairly limited.

I love to upland hunt over our dog and as much as I truly love grouse have always been fascinated by woodcock. Woodcock are very odd little birds (it takes several dozen of them to make a meal for the average adult). They bob along on the ground in damp areas where worms are abundant. Much of their time is consumed with sticking their beaks in the ground in the hope of locating an earthworm bonanza. A biologist friend of mine has told me that they are our slowest-flying game bird and that their brain is upside down and backwards! With an upside-down brain, it's no wonder that I often miss them. If they have no idea what they are doing, how the hell am I supposed to be able to hit them?

As I was about to begin writing about my appreciation of whiskey, enjoyed while drinking from a tin cup, my thought process was interrupted because Lila asked for some help with preparing supper. I bet that when Ernest Hemingway was writing *For Whom the Bell Tolls* he didn't have to go and peel squash!

I have had the very distinct pleasure of enjoying and reveling in the moment of a campfire in the company of great friends while drinking whiskey from a tin cup. There is something about enjoying a recreational beverage, sipped from a tin cup that is very special. Perhaps it was because on many of these moments, I was in an elk camp at eighty-five hundred feet above sea-level, or in a caribou camp on Quebec's Ungava peninsula. Maybe there was a moment in time during one of our many fishing excursions to Chile. I can recall many of these moments in a fishing lodge on the McKenzie River in Labrador, but most of them have been right here in our magnificent state of Maine. Regardless of where we were, there was the pleasure of time spent with dear companions, in the pursuit of whatever the species of the moment happened to be. Truth to tell, I've enjoyed days when we had hot tea warmed over a fire of willow bushes on the tundra of northern Quebec during a caribou hunt that was as enjoyable as the whiskey in the tin cup. Okay, almost as enjoyable!

Another of the great pleasures in my life has been the opportunities to fish beaver bogs. Beaver bogs provide an existence for an amazing amount of various bugs, fish, plants and, of course, beaver. My experience has always been that if you have beaver in a flowage you will also have trout. Beaver bogs are a small version of an eco-system where life in many forms flourishes. My life-long friend, the Kid, and I once drove a 4-wheel drive vehicle up the side of a mountain, where we shouldn't have been walking much less driving. Youth is such an optimistic experience! When we arrived at what we thought was the outlet to a sizeable trout pond, we followed the brook for a couple of hundred yards. When we stepped up to the edge of the water, instead of a pond, we were overlooking a beaver flowage of two or three acres. What made this more interesting was the fact that the surface of this flowage was COVERED with rising trout!

We stood almost mesmerized and just watched for several moments, amazed at our potential good fortune. We remembered that we were there to catch trout and so out came the worms and spinners. This happened in the days when one was allowed eight brook trout. In a matter of minutes, we had eight trout each, ranging from ten to twelve inches. We reveled in our good fortune and headed for the camp, vowing that we'd be back.

Over the next year or two, Kid and I made several visits to this flowage, each time carefully releasing the smaller trout and keeping only a few larger trout. On what would have been our fourth year on this to-die-for spot, we returned in the spring to find that woodcutters had been there the previous fall and had fished the flowage dry and torn out the dam. We were sadly disappointed but have always looked back on two seasons of a simply fabulous fishing experience that included many meals on the shore of the bog, with trout fried in salt pork and cornmeal cooked over an open fire in a big cast-iron skillet. To this day, we talk about those meals, the trout and that spectacular opportunity that we shared.

I have a remarkable affection for eight-inch brook trout. Yes, I have caught brook trout up to ten pounds. Yes, each trout I've caught carries a remarkable memory. But there is something special about a feisty, colorful eight-inch native Maine brook trout that never fails to excite me.

Every once in a while I am in one of those hard to find hidden beaver bogs that I always think that no one else on the planet knows about. I get so excited that my fingers shake as I am tying a fly on the leader. It can't be the size of those bog trout, but pound for pound, they are as exciting to me as one of the Labrador giants. Imagine a world where we didn't have them? I suppose that I'd have to find a way to get excited about smallmouth bass.

I like sunrises and sunsets. If for no other reason than that they remind me that, at least most of the time, my troubles are often not as dire as I had imagined. I love the opening moments of the day as the sun is just peeking over the horizon or the other side of the pond. I can sit there with a cup of coffee and watch Mother Nature's world wake up and start the day.

I like the sound of running water as it makes its way downstream to the next level. I am always tickled by the gurgle of the water as it makes its way around and over the stones. Speaking of water, I really like rain. I love to lie awake at our camp at night and listen to the rain fall through the trees. Our camp is surrounded by woods and we can enjoy the serenade the rain provides there.

I like Maine's wildlife. Just this morning I was fishing with Lila and a friend. We were on the banks of the Kennebec River and were greeted by a pair of adult eagles. We watched as one of them was flying towards us, clutching a fish in his talons. As we listened to a great deal of screeching, the adult flew into a tall pine just behind us. We looked to see where the ruckus came from and realized that we were staring at an active nest, a hundred feet or so from where we stood. In the nest were another adult and a chick, obviously born earlier this spring. We had the good fortune to watch several trips that each of the adults made, each time delivering a freshly-caught fish to the youngster. We stopped fishing and just stood by and enjoyed this incredible experience. So, add eagles to the list of things that I like.

Bonefish Ed

Lila and I used to market sport-fishing trips in the Florida Keys for a very dear friend of ours who lived in Duck Key. Ed was a retired executive from the Enterprise Car Rental Corporation, and moved to the Keys upon his retirement. We met Ed when I guided him on his first Maine sea-duck hunt. We spent many, many weeks in the Keys with Ed, chasing the tarpon, bonefish, permit and anything else that swam.

Ed was a life-long duck hunter, and often commented how much he missed his duck-hunting days on the bayous of Louisiana, hunting the Mississippi Flyway with his friend. Ed's companion for these hunts was a college friend who was born and raised on the waters and bayous of Louisiana. This fellow was a dyed-in-the-wool Cajun in each and every sense of the word, and his name was Thiboudeau. He and Ed were very close friends and he was forever reminding Ed that he should have been born a Cajun. He went so far as to anoint Ed with a Cajun name, always referring to him as "Boudreau."

Ed always laughed as he'd describe the first call from Thiboudeau as fall was approaching. Ed would pick up the phone and he always heard the same thing; "Boudreau, dis' be Thiboudeau on de bayou, grab your twice-barrel shoot gun and get yo'self down hea', dem docks is on de' bayou!" Ed always had Labrador Retrievers in those days and he'd load dog, "twice-barrel shoot guns," all his gear and head for the bayou.

Each fall, Ed would get after Thiboudeau that he needed to buy a duck dog. After several years of procrastination, one evening Ed's phone rang and sure enough, it was Thiboudeau. The first thing that Ed heard was Thiboudeau, yelling into the phone, "Boudreau, I done got me a dock dawg!" Ed was surprised but congratulated his pal for his purchase. When Ed asked him what kind of dog he had purchased, he replied, "Oh, Boudreau, I done got me a fahn duck dawg, I got me a genuine "Laboratory RE-triever!"

After discussing the dog's merits for a few minutes, Ed asked what the dog's name was. His friend replied that he had given the dog a real, honest to God, Cajun name. When he told Ed that the dog's name was Fido, Ed's reaction was to say that half of the mongrel dogs in America were named Fido and what the hell kind of name was Fido for a duck dog? Thiboudeau's reply was, "Oh no, Boudreau, you don't be unnerstan', the dawg have him a fahn Cajun name. I give this a lot of thought, the dawg's name be Fido spelled, PHYDEAUX, FiDo." Ed was forced to admit that his friend had indeed given his "Laboratory Retriever" a fine Cajun name.

Our trips to the Keys with Ed always centered on fly fishing for tarpon. One of my lifelong "bucket list" items was to catch a hundred-pound tarpon with a fly rod. While we had many, many other fishing adventures with Ed that involved bonefish and per-mit, a big tarpon was always at the top of my agenda. We fished with Ed for several years and I was never able to close the show when a chance at a big tarpon presented. Fortunately, in 2019, fishing with another guide in the Key Largo area, I managed to get the monkey, or in this case, the tarpon, off my back, a couple of different times.

The story here is that on our very first tarpon excursion with Ed, I cast my fanny off for two days and literally dozens of big tarpon and could not get one to eat that fly! Around noon on the second day, I was frustrated and told Ed and Lila that if one more tarpon refused my fly, I was going to toss out a crab with a spin-ning (wash my mouth out!) rod and finally get a hook into a tar-pon.

About then, Ed mentioned that there was another pod of tar-pon coming our way. I stood on the casting platform of Ed's skiff and as they came by, made what was a pretty good cast, if I do say so, and dropped that big tarpon fly right in front of a huge tarpon. The fish turned, came to the fly, opened his mouth and then bumped the fly with his nose and left it! I made some comment about having had it and I was going for the crab rod.

Lila had been filming this episode with our camcorder. When I put the fly rod down, she put the camera down, picked up my fly rod and made, look out, here it comes, ONE cast and a tarpon that wound up weighing about one hundred and twenty-five pounds ate the fly! The wind blew a loop of fly line around her index finger and when the tarpon yanked on the fly line, she instinctively pulled back and set the hook. The big fish blew up into the air, and Ed looked at me and said that we'd have to unhook the anchor line and follow the tarpon, so that he wouldn't spool Lila. My reply was, "great, when you start the outboard, I'm throwing myself into the prop!"

Fifty-five long minutes later, we touched the leader, which in the Keys is considered landing the fish, and released him to fight another day. It was a long, long flight home.

We lost Ed several years ago, so sad to say. We shared many memorable days on the water with Ed, and he upland hunted two or three times with us here in Maine. When Ed passed, he left us his fly rod, many tarpon and bonefish flies, and he bequeathed his watch to me. I wear it often and it always brings back memories of sunny, beautiful days on the flats at Long Key Bridge, Baya Honda, and the afternoon that Lila hooked a fifteen-foot hammerhead shark!

RIP, Bonefish.........................

In over thirty years as a guide, among my fishing customers I have worked with many people who were trollers. Although fly-fishing is my passion, I have spent countless hours here in Maine and in Quebec trolling for any of several species, often with surprising results.

During our many years at the Broadback River Fishing Camps, we often trolled for walleye or pike. During one of our many visits to the BRFC, a couple from Maine had joined us. He was an ardent fly-fisherman, but she preferred to sit in a boat, read a book and hold a trolling rod in the sincere hope that the fish would leave her alone. On one particular morning, the couple was trolling in their boat alongside Lila and me. Lots and lots of walleye and pike were caught, cleaned and prepared for us to bring home.

The rule of thumb was after the guides had filleted and cleaned the latest day's catch, they would load fish carcasses in large plastic totes, take them up the lake and dump them in the water. The camps were directly across a large cove from where the Broadback River left Lake Assinica so there was a natural current in this part of the lake.

As we trolled along, all of a sudden our guest's wife gave out a yell, saying she had a heavy fish on. We were all trying to give her suggestions about how to carefully play the big fish to the net and it was apparent that she indeed had a large fish on. We surmised that it was a big pike as it wasn't putting up much of a fight but rather a steady but heavy pull. She managed to get the fish to the side of the boat and her husband took a swipe with the net. Rather than take a chance on losing the fish, he just flopped it into the boat right at her feet.

Almost in an instant, she leaned over the side of the boat and began to violently vomit! She was barfing over the side and her husband launched into gales of laughter. He yelled and said, "C'mere, you've gotta' see this!"

We pulled up beside their boat and in the net lay the filleted carcass of a fifteen or so pound pike that another guest had caught that morning, blood, guts and all. She had foul-hooked the remains of the pike. We all found this to be hysterically funny, but it became immediately obvious that she was not sharing in the humor.

Lila and I made a hasty retreat to the far shore. Across the water we could hear her telling her husband exactly what she thought about all this. To make this worse, her tirade was regularly interrupted by another round of vomiting. Need I say that conversation around the dinner table that evening was very limited and mostly consisted of comments of how nice the weather had been that day.

On another walleye trip to a different lodge, again in Quebec, I was accompanied by five gentlemen of the highest moral character. They were my fellow members of the Wardens Worry Social Club (described in another chapter) and the uncle of one of the members. We were staying for a week, catching walleye and pike, with daily bets on the biggest fish of each species.

Jim was with me in our boat and competition was running high as the largest walleye of that day was about three pounds. Suddenly, Jim had a terrific hit on his jig and told me that he had a hell of a fish on. Jim carefully played the fish to the net and as I netted the fish, it was obvious that Jim had a sure thing winner for the daily pool.

I laid it, still in the net, in the bottom of the boat, unhooked it and because the fish was still struggling I said that I would kill it before I put it in the cooler. In the interests of doing that, I grabbed the walleye and slammed it on the bottom of the boat. As I did this, much to our surprise and dismay, the fish bounced into the air and disappeared over the side of the boat!

There was dead silence in the boat for a moment or two. Rightfully so, Jimmy voiced his displeasure with several rather pointed comments about my fish handling skills. All of this was made worse by the fact that later that day, I caught a walleye that was substantially smaller than Jim's but it won the fish pool for that day. Out of embarrassment, I shared my winnings with Jim. To this day, he denies that I did this.

During the Bosebuck Mountain camps days, I was guiding two ladies for a day of trolling for salmon. We were fishing with downriggers and were barely set up when the first rigger that I'd just put down popped. She did a good job of not hurrying the fish, and as it jumped we saw that she was onto a very nice salmon. The fish came to the boat fairly quickly, jumped once, and in the next moment, jumped again. Not unusual salmon behavior, but the difference was that with the second jump, the fish jumped right into the boat. That sure made the task of carefully netting the salmon much easier.

I have always maintained that fishing makes for a sometimes very small world. One summer day, I guided a couple of extremely nice ladies on their first fishing foray to Maine. One was a nurse and the other was a physician at a hospital in New Orleans. I'd spent a week on business in New Orleans in the late seventies and so we had much to talk about. I mentioned that working as a doctor in New Orleans she must have seen about everything under the sun.

She agreed and told me a story about a man who was brought to the ER with a folding knife protruding from the top of his head! He also happened to be carrying a revolver that was so big that it "should have been on wheels!" He later died from his wound, but it made for quite a story.

The following season I guided two couples and as we trolled the lake one of them mentioned New Orleans. That was all I needed to hear and I told them the story about the man with the knife in his head. About the time that I got to the part about the revolver, one of the women piped up and said, "He had a great, big pistol, right?" I was flabbergasted at how she could possibly know this? She explained that her brother was the other doctor working the ER that night. Wow, simply amazing, at the sometimes small world that we live in.

One of my most memorable trolling moments involved a lady from New Jersey. She was an excellent fly fisherman and I had guided her at Bosebuck Camps for three or four years. Ellen was a very interesting woman and had enjoyed a long career as a stock broker working on Wall Street. On September 11, she was in the South Tower when the first hijacked jet hit the North Tower. Thanks to a security guard, she and her colleagues were warned in time to exit the Tower. As they made their way to safety out of the area, she witnessed the collapse of the building.

The last year that Ellen came to Maine she brought an older gentleman with her who was her close friend. She asked me if I would mind taking Andrew out for a day of trolling on Azicohos Lake as he could no longer walk well enough to wade. We had a great day trolling.

As we fished he told me that he had never caught a brook trout that didn't come out of a hatchery. Later in the afternoon, he hooked and landed a beautiful brook trout of about two pounds. He sat in the bow of the boat holding the trout with a curious expression on his face as I took his picture. He looked at the trout for a long moment and said that he guessed that this was about the most important trout that he'd ever caught. He released the trout and said that he was tired and why didn't we call it a day?

The next morning Ellen and Andrew were preparing to leave and she took me aside and thanked me for spending the day with Andrew. She explained that he was dying of cancer and had been given a matter of months to live. Once again, I was blessed to have given a moment to someone that became their "memory-of-a-lifetime" but also enriched mine.

My career as a fly fisherman began many, many years ago. As relayed in another chapter, I caught my first brook trout with a fly rod at the age of ten. I guess I have never looked back from that handsome morning on the Carrabassett River.

My wife and I began Fins and Furs Adventures in January of 1987 with one outfitter, the Broadback River Fishing Camps (BRFC), located in northwestern Quebec. The Broadback River was in those days a fly-fishing only trophy brook fishery. The trout were big, the biggest that we'd ever seen and sometimes tough to catch. At BRFC a trout was not considered a trophy unless it weighed over five pounds.

Lila and I got the big brook trout fever very quickly. As our business grew, big brookies remained our primary focus and selling point. Over the twelve years that we spent working with the BRFC and the crazy Frenchman Richard, we caught and released brook trout that weighed over eight pounds. My readers need to understand that in today's trout fishing world, a brook trout anywhere above five pounds is a hell of a trophy.

As we grew our business we added additional outfitters where we and our customers had access to not only big brook trout but large landlocked salmon also. As years went by and we became more experienced at hooking, landing (and releasing!) these big trout, their size and my big trout fever grew steadily.

About the turn of the century, we became the business representatives for a lodge in Labrador known as Osprey Lodge, another catch & release fishery. Osprey's very justified claim to fame was that Osprey Lake and a couple of surrounding waters were producing brook trout that were among the largest being caught anywhere in the world. The last year that we represented Osprey Lodge, the AVERAGE brook trout released there weighed six pounds, four ounces. These fish were being caught daily and the largest trout that had ever been taken here weighed a few ounces over eleven pounds.

Keep in mind that the all-tackle world record for brook trout was a fish that was caught in 1914 by a Doctor W. H. Cook. His trout was caught at a place called Rabbit Rapids, in the Nipigon River of Ontario, and weighed FOURTEEN POUNDS, EIGHT OUNCES.

Osprey Lake became an annual visit with customers that would accompany us. I realized very early on in our visits that I had a legitimate opportunity to realize one of my bucket-list goals that I had chased for many years. I was determined that I would catch and release back into the waters from whence it came a ten-pound brook trout.

On July 7, 2007, I took a friend with me for a week at Osprey Lake. On the first evening, he and I went to a large dead water that existed at the outlet of Osprey, known as No Name. This dead water was between Osprey Lake and the next lake in the watershed, named Black Fly. Together these are the head waters of the famous Eagle River.

As a good fishing host should, I offered my friend the first cast at the inlet of the large pool. He made ONE CAST and hooked, landed, weighed and released a trout that weighed eight pounds.

After we released his trophy, I stepped to the water's edge, and using a size 10 White Wulff with a 6X tippet, made one cast. Almost immediately, a very large trout took the dry, turned his head and snapped my tippet. Not to be deterred, I tied on another White Wulff and made, you guessed it, one cast. The fly drifted about two feet and disappeared into a very small swirl. When I lifted the tip of the fly rod to set the hook, 100 feet of fly line and another 60 or so feet of backing disappeared.

Understanding this was a very large trout, I let the rod and reel do what they were designed to do. After a few minutes into this, my guide, Roll Vincent, with his very pronounced Labrador accent said, "Jayzus bye, that's a big fish!" At the sixteen-minute mark, my guide held the net as I steered this magnificent trout into the net. We weighed that trout, and I held him upright in the water as he slowly recovered. That magnificent trout let me know he was ready to go as I realized a life-long dream. After several pictures, I released a ten-pound, four-ounce brook trout alive and well into the water. I just stood there with tears in my eyes as I watched this fish swim away.

I have since enjoyed other bucket-list moments in my career as a fly fisherman, including, by the time you read this, the honor of being the very first fly-fisherman to be inducted into the Maine Sports Hall of Fame. I was afforded this honor for my distinction of having held a total of fifty-two world fly fishing records as recorded by the National Fresh Water Fishing Hall of Fame. I also was the 2020 recipient of the Wiggie Robinson Legendary Maine Guide award, being only the ninth person to be so honored. Being accepted into the Maine Sports Hall of Fame was a personal and career honor of epic proportions for me. But watching "Ten-Pound" swim away was breathtaking!

Partridge hunting under any circumstances is a wonderful although often frustrating sport. Add pointing or flushing dogs and the odds of unusual and story-producing moments grow significantly. Introducing woodcock, one of Mother Nature's oddest creations in the world of game birds, only adds to the mix.

Lila and I happen to know three brothers who live in central New York and have been our friends for over thirty years. They began as upland customers when we were the managers at Bosebuck Mountain camps on Azicohos Lake west of Rangeley. Bob, Mike and Craig showed up for several days of upland hunting with us and the rest, as they say, is history. They became, and remain to this day, dear friends with whom we have shared many, many hunting days here in Maine and fishing experiences at their camp on Lake Ontario.

One particular day, we were hunting over our pointing dogs near our West Forks camp. Our male Blackfield, Doc, was on the ground and Doc locked up on a point. I got the boys into a position where they could shoot and moved in to flush the grouse. When the bird lifted off the ground, one of the brothers, who is a notoriously terrible shot, swung and fired. In what was a moment of amazement to the rest of us, the bird folded up and tumbled from the air. Unfortunately, as the grouse came down, he landed precisely on the top of a 15-foot tall popple stub and stayed there. His two brothers and I were laughing convulsively at this unusual, to say the least, and unbelievable turn of events.

One of his brothers is a couple of inches north of 6 feet. With the help of the entire group, I managed to stand on his shoulders and still couldn't reach the bird. Somebody grabbed a long, dead branch and using that, I managed to nudge the dead bird off the top of the tree and to the ground. I remarked that day that if I ever write a book, this is going to be in it. He is still trying to live this down.

For ten wonderful years, we had an English Setter from the Grouse Ridge line named Sam, short for Samantha. Sam was without question one of the finest pointing dogs that we will ever hunt over. She taught Lila and me a great deal about upland hunting and was always very insistent that we hold up our end of the bargain. In other words, she had little or no patience when we missed and, at the least, would give us the evil eye if we didn't connect.

On one occasion at Bosebuck Camps, Sam and I had the day off and were scouting a new area. As we were making our way back to my truck, we came down a stretch of a very old woods road that had begun to grow up with young firs, two to three feet tall. Sam was ahead of me in the road and all of a sudden stopped and froze with her nose pointing at a small clump of these firs. I took one step and tucked in between the little firs was a handsome cock partridge.

The road was clear ahead of me and there were very few trees to either side. I realized that I had a clear shot in any direction and so I made a "cluck" noise which was Sam's signal to take a few steps and flush the bird. Sam did exactly what she was supposed to do and as she took a step, the bird roared off the ground. I swung my Ruger twenty-guage and pulled the trigger twice.

The bird was apparently living a charmed life because I never so much as broke a feather. The partridge sailed off into the woods, unscathed, and I looked at Sam. She watched the bird for a moment or two, and then swung her head, stared at me for several seconds, and then turned and walked back up the road, going in the direction she'd just come from! She clearly was frustrated with my lack of accuracy and wanted nothing more to do with me just then. She got a hundred or so yards up the road from me and showed no signs of coming back until I gave in. So I pulled out my whistle and gave her a recall blast. We were about fifteen minutes from the truck and she never left the road again.

That evening, I brought her into our camp and made nice with her, asking for her forgiveness. I'm quite sure that her confidence in my shooting ability was at an all-time low. Sam, Lila and I went on to have many more memorable moments and successful hunts.

During our 25-year run with the Blackfield Pointers, for 12 of the final 16 years, Doc was our rock star. His ticking was orange, and he sired several litters with our Kate, who was the love of Doc's life. Doc was a very large pointer, weighing nearly 80 pounds and had one blue and one brown eye. This gave him a rather distinctive look and he played the role very well.

Doc was undoubtedly one of the very best pointers that we have had the honor of hunting over. But his methods, as good and steady as he was, were sometimes a bit unusual. Doc's method of moving through the woods was what Lila and I always referred to as "the ax and smash method". Doc wasn't much for going around things. When he decided that the birds were in the thick covers, he'd just simply run over or more often through things. The result of this approach was that often by the day's end, he'd be pretty beaten up—nose bloody, tail raw, and chest all scratched up. But this never bothered him much. I had the honor of being this dog's human for 12 years and we had an incredible journey together.

Over the years with many of our upland hunting customers, Doc earned quite a reputation as an excellent upland dog and was quite a character. Part of Doc's fame produced some national publicity.

One summer, I received a call from an acquaintance of ours who was an LL Bean employee. He explained that Bean's wanted a guide and an upland dog for a commercial shoot which would take place in Freeport. Not only would Doc and I get some serious publicity, but we would be very well compensated for our time. With no hesitation, I jumped at the opportunity and immediately let Lila and some of our friends know that Doc and I would be featured in a big-time television commercial.

On the appointed day, Doc and I made our way to Freeport, looking our very best, of course, and ready for stardom. We reported to the site of the shoot, which was located near a field adjacent to a wooded area with the bay in the background. Sad to say, my dreams of added fame were dashed when they passed me the check for services rendered and told me that Doc and a professional model were to be the featured stars of the commercial. They didn't want me after all; they just wanted the damn dog! Doc's fame continued to grow while I was relegated to being his straight man.

Doc's very first actual hunt was in New Brunswick in the alder and poplar covers on the banks of the beautiful Renous River. I'd shot quail and pigeons for him (which he hated and refused to retrieve), but this was his first official hunt. We were with George Curtis who owned Black Rapids Lodge in Blackville, NB. We were marketing Atlantic salmon business for George, so he invited us over for an upland hunt. With me were Harry Vanderweide, editor of the *Maine Sportsman* and host of the TV show, "The Maine Sportsman," and his videographer, Joe Saltalamachia.

We pulled up to the first cover of the day and I let Doc out of the dog box. I turned to grab my gun and when I looked back, Doc was on the far side of an apple tree, solid on a point. It took me a second to recover just because here we were on his first hunt, and in less than 20 seconds, he's on point! Harry scored as the woodcock flushed and went out of sight beyond the apple tree.

I released Doc and he went on to retrieve the bird, or so I hoped. Doc went out of sight momentarily and then came bounding back to me, with at first glance, no bird. Doc had very large floppy jowls. I stood there assuming that he, lacking any actual hunting experience other than his training sessions, hadn't recovered the woodcock.

As he neared me, I looked again and out from the back corners of his mouth protruded 2 little woodcock legs. He had picked up the bird, held the entire bird, excluding the legs, in his mouth and delivered it into my hand with not so much as a feather broken. This began a long and fabulous career with Doc. He was an inherently funny dog and made us laugh constantly.

As it always seems with hunting dogs, eventually we came to Doc's last hunt.

He had begun to have difficulty walking and getting around in the covers. He and I were in a cover together in West Athens, just the two of us. We were in an alder cover that was across a field from the road. Doc and I had hunted this cover many, many times over the years and he knew it like the back of his paw. He pointed a woodcock and I killed it.

When Doc went into the brush to pick up the bird, he got his back legs hung up and fell down. He had quite a time to get back on his feet and finally brought the bird to me.

At that specific moment, I knew that this would be his last hunt. It broke my heart to see this magnificent hunting dog, who was so dear to me, no longer able to be in the covers without being in danger of hurting himself.

I took the woodcock from him and we walked across the field to the truck. I cried all the way across the field. When we reached the truck, I had to help him into the front seat with me, which is where he rode when it was just the two of us. Doc never hunted again, but he remained my constant companion. I kept hoping that he would just lie down and go to sleep before the next fall came around.

October came and he was still with us and upland season was here. I was loading the other Blackfields into the dog boxes (Doc was the only one of the dogs who got to ride in the front seat), and I couldn't look at him. Nothing that has ever happened with all of the hunting dogs that we've had over all these years has ever hurt me as much as driving away leaving Doc in the kennel watching.

Rest in peace my friend. One of these days we'll be in the covers together again and those birds will be in trouble.

This is yet another story that stems from the ongoing competition that Lila and I have when it comes to our hunting, fishing, and of course cribbage playing activities. The story began earlier in the year while in the Florida Keys on a tarpon fishing trip with our dear friend there, Ed Bayer (see the chapter entitled Bonefish Ed). On this trip Lila happened to be the first in our family to catch a tarpon on a fly.

On this particular November day, Lila and I were deer hunting in a wooded area about ten miles from our home. We moved through a wooded area that had deer signs everywhere and clear indications that a big buck was working the area. We left the woods to cross a field and as we neared the other side, Lila happened to glance over her shoulder. As she did this, there running across the side of the field that we'd just left, was a tremendous buck deer. She was really caught unawares by the sight of this terrific deer and was, for a moment, speechless.

When she could speak, she said, "Holy shit, look at that buck!" Now, when it comes to my deer hunting, I have always been pretty quick on the shoot, and this was no exception. When she yelled, I spun around, took three or four steps to the side to be positive that I was well away from her, threw up my gun and killed the buck in his tracks. She looked at me and said, "You shot my buck!" I looked back at her with a big grin on my face and said, "Nice tarpon, huh?" It was fairly quiet for a minute of two and then we both started to laugh. She finally admitted I had exacted my revenge.

I field-dressed the buck and we pulled him off the ridge to our truck. The deer had a huge frame, with antlers to match. He had fourteen countable points and measured twenty-three inches inside his antlers. After drying for the proper period, I asked a scorer from the Maine Antler and Skull Trophy Club to measure the antlers and the final score was one-hundred, forty-six MASTC points, meaning that I was well over the minimum of one hundred forty.

The only thing that this buck lacked was pounds. His body was huge, but he had apparently been "entertaining" his lady friends and had worn himself down to skin and bone. In these travels I was not, apparently, the first to make a shot on him either. In his left ear there was a hole about the diameter of a .30 caliber projectile.

The body of this deer was much larger than "Dementia buck," mentioned in another chapter. The Holy Shit Buck now graces the wall in our living room, along with Dementia buck, and I have been forced to admit that Lila did spot this trophy first. In my mind that makes us even because I spotted her tarpon first. We both took one for the team.

I have hunted deer or at the least wandered aimlessly in the woods since the fall that I was three. One of the two earliest memories of my life as a child goes back to that first fall, walking in the woods with my dad while he deer hunted. I remember that we heard someone shoot nearby and Dad told me to get on the ground. Little did I realize that this was the beginning of my life-long pursuit of one of Mother Nature's most magnificent creatures, the whitetail deer. Since that significant day, I have spent what are certainly tens of thousands of hours, and a vast fortune, in my pursuit of deer, especially big bucks. It's also worth noting that since that day with my dad, I have never through the entire month of November drawn a restful breath.

Like many hunters, my continued efforts with deer hunting almost always had an emphasis on putting meat in the freezer. However, there was a nagging shadow of having either or both of two shirt patches. One would be for Biggest Bucks in Maine Club (BBMC), requiring a deer that field dressed over 200 pounds, and the other for the Maine Antler & Skull Trophy Club (MASTC), which requires a buck with antlers that, when measured, would score a minimum of one hundred and forty points.

As a young man, I kept thinking, "How tough can this be?" But as the years continued to slip by and I kept coming up short, the cold hard facts began to sink in. Over the years, I saw several deer that would have qualified for either patch, and in a few cases for both of these patches. But somehow, I never seemed to manage to close the show. Not that I didn't harvest a number of very nice bucks.

In the case of the BBMC, I took bucks with dressed weights of 194½, 190, 188, 184, and others of similar size but never was successful in reaching the ultimate goal. And even though I also had deer with beautiful antlers, 8-9-11 points, they still came up short. I continually looked to my left when I should have looked right, or walked when I should have been motionless, or worst case, I just plain missed.

One fall, I had a running shot at a huge-bodied buck with massive antlers at about 40 yards. I swung the rifle, settled the crosshairs with what I thought was a perfect lead, and squeezed the trigger. My lead was perfect, and he should have been dead. Unfortunately, when I fired I shot directly into the middle of a 10" fir tree that I never saw!

Through my forties and fifties, the bucks came and went, unfortunately unscathed. Once I was sitting just over the top of a ridge that was loaded with beechnuts. I was using a pair of deer antlers from an earlier season and by rattling the antlers, tried to imitate two bucks fighting, I hoped that another buck would hear the racket and think that he could sneak in and speed a doe away while the boys duked it out, deer-fashion.

I'd rattled the antlers and blew on my grunt tube, and from over the top of the ridge, a buck answered with a grunt of his own. After a half-hour of grunting back and forth and rattling, something didn't seem just right. I snuck up to the top and peeked over the crest of the ridge. Much to my dismay (and embarrassment) there sat another hunter, doing exactly the same thing that I was. We both apologized and moved on to greener pastures.

Mercifully, in 1997, my fortunes changed. On November 17, with the temperature at 70 degrees, Lila and I were walking across a plowed field looking ahead to an old apple orchard where we planned to sit for the last hour or two of the hunting day. Lila happened to look back over her shoulder at the field that we'd just crossed and said excitedly, "Holy shit, look at that buck!"

I spun around and with Lila standing right beside me, we were shocked to see a deer with massive antlers trying to sneak behind us, running across the field. I took two fast steps to my right, with the buck at full run, and snapped off my shot. The buck went down face first, dead when he hit the ground. This deer had a huge body and big wide antlers, and as I pulled the trigger, I just knew that I had harvested a buck that would bring me not one but both of the patches that I had pursued for so many years.

We walked across the field and as we neared the buck, I realized that I could count every one of his ribs. Much to my dismay, this deer was emaciated and just skin and bones. The previous summer had been extremely dry and, as a result, we had very few apples, and virtually no beechnuts or acorns. To make things worse, when we backtracked the deer to see where he'd come into the field, it was obvious that he had been keeping company with three or four does who had apparently kept him very busy, whispering sweet nothings into his ear. Limited food conditions coupled with the fact that buck deer in November are exactly like I was when I was 18, had kept the old boy pretty lean.

When we got to the tagging station and weighed him, he tipped the scales at 194 pounds. Talk about mixed emotions! I had shot the buck of my lifetime, speaking in terms of antler scores, but my search for the BBMC deer continued. As it turned out, this buck scored 146 ½ which qualified me for my MASTC patch. One down and one to go.

Fast-forwarding twenty years to November of 2016 found me hunting in the area around our camp, which is located in the West Forks in northern Somerset County. My good friend Adam and I each had a young Labrador retriever. We'd come to the camp area in hopes of finding grouse for them and, because it was November and deer season was in full swing, I couldn't stand not to bring a deer rifle. I'd brought my Browning .308, in the event that the dumbest buck in Maine stepped into the dirt road.

We took what is called the Smith Pond Road, heading east from Johnson Mountain and Route 201. As we made our way across the old road, we were focusing on birds for the dogs and I really was unprepared for what came next. We turned the corner and standing at 70 yards, apparently unconcerned about us, was a huge buck. I stepped out of the truck, ran the bolt on the Browning forward and then put the clip in the gun. The loading was done very precisely and quickly, except for one teensy detail. In order for the bolt to move the round forward into the chamber, one must insert the clip into the receiver first.

I put the cross hairs on the buck's chest and squeezed the trigger. My trigger pull was followed by a click, accompanied by dead silence. In the meantime, the deer that will always to be known to my wife and friends, especially Adam who sat watching this performance, as Dementia Buck, waited patiently while I ran another round into the chamber and pulled the trigger.

Dementia dropped where he stood and as we rushed up to him, it was obvious that I had killed a buck with a very large body. We field dressed him and drove to Berry's Store where we tagged and then weighed the buck. Once the scales settled down, as I held my breath, I realized that I had my BBMC buck and the second patch of my quest was mine. I wear both patches on my Johnson green and black wool hunting jacket. When I am asked to tell my story about this deer, I simply say, "200 pounds, one-shot kill at 70 yards" and leave the rest to the imagination.

Lila's very first deer kill was during the second fall that we were together. She'd hunted quail with her dad in Georgia but hadn't ever hunted deer. Getting tangled up with me meant that she was going to become a deer hunter.

During our pre-deer season travels through the woods, one of the things that I taught her was that most things that you see in the woods are vertical. I added that as she moved through the woods, she should look for things that were horizontal, for example a deer's body as it stood wherever it was. Once she found something that fit the horizontal description, then begin to look for ears, noses or antlers.

A cold Saturday morning found us in an area that had a long stretch of hardwoods that gradually sloped downhill into a large bog. The plan was that she would walk along through the hardwood area and I would stay down in the bog, moving in the same direction in the hope that I could push a deer or two by her.

I was part way up the valley, and I heard her shoot. No one was more excited than I was, thinking how wonderful it was that she'd had a chance to shoot at deer on our first day in the woods together. As I started to make my way up the slope to the area where I knew she'd be, I suddenly heard a second, but very muffled, gun shot.

When you are dispatching a wounded deer, in the interests of making a humane and ethical harvest, you hold the muzzle close to the animal. When the weapon is fired, rather than a typical loud bang, the sound is more of a "whump." As I heard the first, and typically only, whump I was even more excited to think that she'd actually harvested her first deer.

But, the plot thickened suddenly, because I heard a second whump. Wondering what the hell happened, I hurried over the crest of the ridge and a hundred or so yards away, there was Lila, obviously very excited and standing over her first whitetail deer.

As I reached her, she explained that the second whump was, because she was using a scoped weapon, she put the muzzle on the deer's neck and tried to look through the scope when she pulled the trigger. And because she was so nervous, she missed. Somewhere between the gales of laughter, I mentioned that it amazed me that she could hit the deer from over a hundred yards away, shooting through the woods but miss from three inches away!

In the span of the years that I have lived, I have had the distinct privilege of knowing an astounding number of people, both men and women, who were unique to say the least. They were often people from my parents' generation who grew up in a world that is vastly different from the world that we have today. These people were mostly teachers, hunters, fishermen and people who lived from the land. The tough world that they lived and worked in was long ago and is gone forever. I was thinking the other day about some of the endless numbers of their old-time "recipes" for almost anything, as my grandfather used to say, that ailed you. For example, a cure for bee stings was to put tea bags in very hot water, make a poultice out of them and put this, as hot as you could stand it, on the sting.

My grandmother's recipe for cooling yourself down when the weather was hot and sticky was to hold your wrists under cold running water, the trick being that the water ran over the pressure points in your wrist and "cooled your blood."

Uncle Bill's recipe for "fly dope" (insect repellant) was to mix Johnson's baby oil, oil of tar, and citronella. You could always tell when you were around someone who used it, as they smelled a little pungent. But it worked.

If you mix lighter fluid in a small glass bottle and add Gulf wax (paraffin) by shaving the wax into the fluid until the fluid won't dissolve any more wax, you have an excellent dry fly floatant. This is all I have used for 35 years and it works as well as, or better, than any of the commercial dry fly solutions.

Pre-paint an aluminum boat with vinegar so that the new paint will stick.

Turpentine and lard mixed and applied to your chest, then covered with a warm flannel cloth, will fight chest colds. The turpentine is an aromatic and the lard keeps it from burning the skin. The warm flannel cloth is just heavenly.

My grandmother's recipe to treat a cough was to mix molasses, onions, sugar, a pat of butter, and vinegar. I still use this to this day simply because it works.

There are a million of these home remedies for many, many uses. The unique thing about these various recipes is that they worked, and you could make them at home. They were concocted from trial and error recipes that were passed down from generation to generation, because someone had a need for a specific product or use.

Truthfully, it makes me sad to think that our world has evolved to the point where many of these recipes and so many others are now forever lost. I suppose that progress and the way of civilization is inevitable, but I still use these old-time remedies whenever I can. Using them makes me feel somehow connected to a time that is otherwise gone forever.

I have always been the first to willingly acknowledge that I am a lucky SOB to be married to my wife Lila. For the record, she is regarded as the CEO, CFO, and the person who is typically considered to be in charge at Fins and Furs Adventures.

We met in September of 1980. I was employed as a purchasing agent by a major construction company that was rebuilding a paper mill in Madison, Maine. Our purchasing secretary and Lila were great friends, and she introduced us. In that first meeting, Lila had interviewed for a position as an executive secretary with the CEO of the mill. Consequently, she was dressed to the nines in business-like attire and simply beautiful.

However, in a few days she showed up at our office again, as beautiful as ever, on her way to meet a fellow that she was dating. She wore a red and gold flannel shirt, jeans, boots and a red bandanna in her hair. She looked sensational, but what drove me crazy was the fact that she was carrying a fly rod. We exchanged pleasantries and she left to meet her date. I was out of my mind. This beautiful woman was a fly fisherwoman. Her favorite body fragrance was Old Woodsman fly dope.

At this particular point in my life, I had just initiated the legal process to divorce my daughter's mother after several years of unhappy times for both of us. The absolute last thing that I wanted or expected was to begin another relationship with anyone that lasted longer than breakfast the next morning.

I drove our secretary nuts asking her to get me Lila's phone number. After confirming that I had in fact filed for a divorce, Lila gave the secretary permission to give me her phone number.

Our romance began with a call every evening to chat and get to know each other a bit. We finally agreed that our first date would be a day of fly fishing. I picked her up at five-thirty in the morning and we spent a spectacular day getting to know each other, just talking and laughing. We fished the Kennebec in the area around the West Forks and we spent the last hour there with our waders off, sitting on the riverbank, "sozzling" our feet in the water and talking. Somewhere in that conversation, I leaned over and kissed her and guess what? She blushed. The day went on and I hoped it wouldn't end.

Finally, I took her home and we agreed that we would see each other again the following weekend. I have never been a true believer in love at first sight, and to this day, I don't know that that was what happened to me. But I can tell you that when I left her at ten p.m. that first evening, the last thing that I said was, "Look, you do realize that this is not going to end here, don't you?" To this day, we talk about that evening and laugh about her reply. She came back with the classic, female, no-comment reply, saying, "Well, okay, we'll see, probably, maybe, you can call me!"

Since that day forty-one years ago, we have never once looked back and questioned that this particular day was one of the most significant days of our lives. We have built a business, have a home that is for the first time really a home full of love, and in simplest terms, have spent the last forty-one years laughing.

If there is a common thread beyond that we love each other like crazy, it has been laughter. We both possess a very significant sense of humor and have played some unusual to say the least, practical jokes on each other. The year that she turned forty she was commuting daily to Augusta, our state capital. This meant a two-way ride daily up and down Interstate 95.

That morning, unbeknownst to her, I snuck out before she left and taped a sign to the rear of her vehicle, reading, "Honk, I'm forty!" After she came home that night (and was speaking to me again), she recounted about how car after car passed her and waved. One guy in a truck passed her, let her go by him and then passed her again honking and waving.

As you might guess, the practical joke practice quickly became a two-way street. During the period when we were the General Managers at Bosebuck Mountain Camps, west of Rangeley, she got me with a beauty. It was November and deer season was at full throttle. We had an errand to run in Rangeley and naturally we brought a gun with us.

I had just finished five straight days of guiding 4 deer hunters. They had been a handful and at the end of their stay, I was exhausted. Lila graciously (or so I thought) offered to drive us into town and I could ride shotgun in the event that we saw a deer. We weren't far along on the thirteen-mile drive to the main road and I was out like a light, gun in my lap when she sprung the trap. All of a sudden, she started yelling at the top of her lungs, "deer, deer, right there, there he is!"

I went from a dead sleep to instant panic. Cartridges went flying everywhere, I was frantically trying to grasp the door handle, and I nearly dropped the gun. Lila was laughing so hard that she had to stop the truck and get out. In the span of three seconds, I went from unconscious to frantic alert. It took me a few seconds to realize that she had gotten her revenge. We still laugh about that to this day.

She and I are extremely competitive in most things that we do. In particular, we have a very active rivalry when it comes to our hunting and fishing. The fact that our business allows us to travel to areas where hunting and fishing are spectacular, has helped to fuel the competition.

One fall a number of years ago during our November deer season, we each harvested an 8-point buck on the same day and nearly simultaneously. The competition was immediately on as we took the deer to the tagging station not just to tag them, but more importantly, to weigh them. When we got both deer on the scales, I found out, to my dismay, that her buck was six pounds heavier than mine.

I suppose it goes without saying that the next twelve months were the longest year of my life. Don't ask me how, but I got cards from customers in New York saying, "So, we heard Lila's buck was bigger than yours!" Wonder how they found that out?

Lila is the easiest woman on the earth to shop for. Flowers and wine are great, but more typically its fly rods, guns and outdoor gear. The very first gift that I bought for her was a new shotgun. Hey, we're talking romance here!

I was so proud of her when, at the age of fifty-four, she received her bachelor's degree in Business Management. But no more so than the day that she became a Master Maine Guide.

I am sure that Lila will agree that over the last forty-one years there have been very few dull moments. I cannot begin to imagine how my life would have been so different, nor can I imagine life without her.

Our career as business owners has taken us all over Robin Hood's barn, on two continents. We've traveled from Chile and Argentina, Cuba, throughout the Caribbean, Florida Keys, west to elk country, and literally all over Eastern Canada. Most of the time, she has patiently allowed me to haul her all over creation. Although, there was that time in Chile when we were stuck in an airport smaller than the airport in Norridgewock, Maine. The nearest community was (or has been) a village named Chaiten. This was the town that had been destroyed by a volcano eruption a matter of weeks after we finally got out of there.

I have never said this before publicly, but the honest-to-God truth is that we have never had an argument. Never! This is not to say that we always agree, because we certainly don't. We have a tremendous amount of respect for each other and our opinions. When we differ, we respectfully state our opinion and then just let it go. I jokingly say that sometimes she is right and sometimes I am right when she says I can be.

The truth is that we are a team and are very good together at what we do.

As you now understand, the title for this book came from many misadventures that always seemed to find me on the wrong side of the river, literally and otherwise. I was often on the opposite side of where the fish were, and where I should have been. But on September 8th, 1986, after years of not being where I wanted to be, I finally made it to the right side of the river and have been ever since.

Everybody loves Lila! Did I mention that I am the luckiest SOB on this planet?

About the Author

Carroll caught his very first brook trout at the tender age of ten. He always maintained from the moment that 10-inch brook trout took the Parmachenee Belle fly, he and the trout were hooked! Carroll comes from several generations of outdoorsmen and women, hunters, fishermen, Guides and schoolteachers.

Initially licensed in 1989 as a Master Maine Guide, Carroll spent the next 33 years guiding hunters and fishermen in the great state of Maine and various destinations in Quebec. Carroll's wife of 40+ years is also a lifelong outdoorsman, a Master Maine Guide, and a natural to keep pace with him.

Together, Carroll and Lila operate Fins & Furs Adventures. They provide worldwide fishing and hunting opportunities, and have taken clients to various locations in North and South America. For over thirty years, they have conducted programs for people who want to obtain their Maine Guide's license.

The year 2020 was large for Carroll. First, Carroll received the Department of Inland Fisheries & Wildlife's prestigious Legendary Maine Guide award. He was inducted into the Maine Sports Hall of Fame as the first fly fisherman in no small part due to amassing 52 World Fly Fishing Records through the Fresh Water Fishing Hall of Fame.

This book of true stories comes directly from Carroll's lifetime in the outdoors.